GW01091421

Plate 1.   The Parsonage today.

Haworth Parsonage

The home of the Brontës
by
JOCELYN KELLETT

The Brontë Society, 1977

Contents

Printed by Fretwell & Brian Ltd., Howden Road, Silsden, Keighley, W. Yorks.

ISBN 0 9505829 0 5

Introduction

1777 was an important year in the history of the Brontës. This was the year Patrick Brontë was born in Emdale, County Down, and the year in which plans to build the new parsonage in Haworth began to take shape. The records show that by 1778 the building of the house was already going ahead, but another 42 years were to pass before Patrick Brontë came to the house which was to be his home until he died in 1861.

Members of the Brontë Society in 1974 subscribed to a fund to acknowledge their debt to our illustrious and devoted Past-President, Dr. Donald Hopewell, whose services to the Society are widely known. When he was asked to what purpose this fund should be put he generously offered it towards defraying the cost of this publication. The book, therefore, is primarily intended as a record of the early history of the house, together with a background of the domestic life of the Brontës in the period 1820 to 1861 and secondly, as a tribute to Dr. Hopewell in recognition of his service and devotion to Brontë scholarship. 1977 is the bi-centenary of the birth of Patrick Brontë and the birth of the idea which culminated in the now famous Brontë Parsonage. A fitting occasion to pay tribute to those who helped to make this house famous.

Work done on the Parsonage previously has only been recorded in a fragmentary way, and no collated account has been available to anyone interested in the history of the house and its contents. Early accounts of the Brontës deal, for the most part, with their literary attainments. The details and influence of their home seem to have been of no interest. It was felt that this was an opportune time to publish a printed record of these changes and, at the same time, to give an account of the life style of the Brontë family.

Sale catalogues, diaries and notebooks of the Brontës, and accounts, are to be found at the Museum together with detailed copies of the plans. The church warden's account is to be found at Bradford Central Library, wills and terrier at the Borthwick Institute, title deeds at Wakefield Registry of Deeds. Further information has been made available by the Trustees of Church

Lands. The Archives Department of Leeds City Library made available the plans of the Tithe Award and the Keighley Rate Office supplied valuable help on Mr. Brontës' tax returns. Many other libraries made material available for research in the early history of the land purchase. To all these I owe my thanks.

In addition, I would like to thank Dr. Eric Gee of the Royal Commission on Historical Monuments for his help in assessing the architectural features of the house, and Arthur Hartley for his ever willing assistance with building technicalities. Many friends in the Society have given encouragement and advice, but foremost amongst these is Amy Foster. Her expertise in guiding me through the maze of documentation and her determination in pursuit of early records, frequently, alas, not to be discovered, has made the chapter on the early history possible.

The book falls into three parts. The beginning deals with the acquisition and building of the house, the middle gives architectural details and the end gives an account based on writings of the Brontës which indicate the way of life in their household.

I hope this work does something to show how the family lived in the home they loved so well and to dispel some of the gloom which has been cast around them.

JOCELYN KELLETT.
February, 1977.

Useful Dates and References

Unless otherwise stated, references are drawn from the following sources and indicated by initials.

B.C.L. Bradford City Library. The Heaton Papers.

B.P.M. Brontë Parsonage Museum.

B.S.T. Brontë Society Transactions.

C.C. The Church Commissioners, formerly known as Queen Anne's Bounty.

C.S. Clement Shorter "The Brontës, Life and Letters" published Hodder and Stoughton 1908. Letter number given.

E.C.G. "The Life of Charlotte Brontë" by E. C. Gaskell, published by John Grant 1924, Edinburgh.

S.H.B. "The Brontës: Their lives, friendships & correspondence in four volumes." Published Oxford 1932 Shakespeare Head Press. Letter number given.

T.C.L. Trustees for Church Lands.

List of Illustrations

Acquiring the Parsonage

The first Annual Meeting of the Brontë Society was held on December 8th, 1894 at Dewsbury Town Hall under the presidency of Sir John Brigg of Kildwick Hall. There were 163 Members, the annual subscription was 2/6d, and their aim was to gather together and house "personal relics of the unique family of Haworth". These were housed in a room above the Yorkshire Penny Bank in Main Street, Haworth and the Museum was opened there on May 18th, 1895. The opening ceremony was a red letter day in Haworth. The *Bradford Observer* recounts how special trains were laid on, the pavements scrubbed, flags hung out and the houses spotless, ham teas were provided with a liberality which astonished those unaccustomed to West Riding hospitality. At a meeting in May, 1894, the paper recorded that £300 would be enough to "acquire practically the whole of the available relics of the Brontë family".

Seven years later moves were already afoot to obtain the Parsonage as the obvious house for a Brontë Museum. The house belonged, as has been said, to the Trustees of Church Lands, not to the Church Commissioners and the incumbent the Rev. John Wade was not unwilling to move if suitable accommodation could be provided for his family. He had felt, like Mr. Brontë, incommoded by the enthusiasts who were anxious to see the home of the famous sisters. The project however was a long delayed one and it was many years before it was achieved.

Sir James Roberts, a native of Haworth and Lady Roberts were two of many who wished to see these relics return to their original home at the Parsonage, and it was through their generosity and forethought that this came about. In 1928 arrangements were completed with the Church Commissioners and the Church Trustees whereby another rectory was provided for the incumbent and the Brontë Society was given the Haworth Parsonage. On August 4th, 1928 Sir James Roberts, who had purchased the Parsonage, handed over the Deeds to the President, Sir Edward (later Lord) Brotherton, before a huge crowd which included many distinguished literary figures.

7

Thousands of visitors, including many Americans and residents of Haworth, thronged the streets to be present. Sir James Roberts in his address spoke of hearing "Mr. Brontë preach in the pathetic blindness of his old age". He had known Mr. Nicholls and Martha Brown and remembered Charlotte. Sir Edward Brotherton expressed the thanks of the Society which now had 350 members and said the building "lends itself admirably to the purpose for which we desire it". After messages from Lord Haldane and Sir William Watson, Lady Roberts opened the door of the Parsonage and the Leeds architect W. A. Ledgard presented her with a gold key. Sir Edward Brotherton placed a wreath of heather on the Brontë grave and "the party of distinguished guests adjourned to the Black Bull where they were entertained to tea by the President." (1)

The house was large (too large for the small number of exhibits the Society had at that time to display), but the hard work and enthusiasm of the band of workers reaped an unexpected and valuable reward. Mr. Henry H. Bonnell of Philadelphia bequeathed his magnificent collection of Brontëana to be housed at the Museum, and Mrs. Bonnell came from the United States with valuable suggestions about its arrangement.

The Society again had cause to be thankful for the generosity of its Patrons, not only for the gifts of money, but because many more items were offered and it was at this time that the nucleus of the Museum as we know it today was laid down. Since then, many more items have been acquired and the greatest care has always been taken to establish their authenticity. One of the most useful acquisitions in this respect was the original catalogue of the sale at the Parsonage on October 1st and 2nd 1861. After Mr. Brontë died, Mr. Nicholls left the Parsonage returning to his native Ireland taking many relics with him, but leaving the rest to be put up for auction. The sale catalogue gives a list of the purchasers and the price paid. This little book has been invaluable in tracing the provenance of articles and although description of each item is teasingly short, to have the name of the original purchaser has been useful in checking authenticity. Visitors to the Museum and members, can be assured that every care is taken and many items have, regretfully, had to be rejected because their authenticity could not be firmly established. After Mr. Nicholls' death other items were put up for sale at Sotheby's. Many of these were known to have belonged to the Brontë family and were bought for the

Museum. Any exhibit today at the Parsonage which did not belong to the Brontës is clearly so labelled.

In 1974, 200,000 visitors passed through this comparatively small Museum. The problem this presents is one that requires ingenuity and patience if each visitor is to be able to examine the items on display without wear and tear on the fabric of an old house becoming too great. The Council of the Society is aware of its responsibilities to the public and to the valuable material of which it is custodian. In 1976 a strongroom of the latest type, with temperature and humidity control, was installed at considerable cost. The increasing value placed on Brontë manuscripts made this investment essential. Modern methods of reproducing manuscripts allow exact copies to be placed on view as it would be unwise to display fragile originals which are subject to deterioration by light, damp or excessive dryness.

The Site of the Parsonage

Haworth Church Land Trustees

Few records are extant for compiling a history of the Parsonage owing to the unique arrangement made for the maintenance of the incumbent of the church.

The Patron of the living of Haworth was the Vicar of Bradford. Haworth was a parochial chapelry and its parson a perpetual curate until 1867 when, a separate District having been assigned to it in 1864, the District Chapelry was made a Rectory.

The chief source of the curate's income came from a 14th century endowment of a chantry chapel in the church and when chantries were dissolved in 1547 this income was lost. The inhabitants, with characteristic independence, collected £36, bought three (later increased to five) farms in Stanbury and created a Trust. The Trustees, freeholders of Haworth, were appointed by a deed of 18th December 1559 and were known as The Trustees for Church Lands. They were to administer the Stanbury Estate and pay the rents and profits to a minister "who doth the usual duties of Divine Service in the Chappel of Haworth", but with a proviso that if the Trustees "be debarred in their choice or in the nomination of a minister when any vacancy shall happen" they had the power to withold the income. This clause, which still operates, has been the cause of several disputes over the years, and explains the Trustees' refusal to accept the Patron's choice of Samuel Redhead in 1819 and the eventual acceptance of Mr. Brontë. The existence of the Trust explains the paucity of records. The Trustees acting independently of the Archbishop, made no application for a faculty for building and consequently there are no relevant records in the Diocesan Registry, nor have the Trustees preserved any building accounts.

An example of how the Trustees worked is seen in the letter Mr. Brontë wrote to the Secretary of the National School Society when acknowledging a gift of £80 towards the building costs of a school on land belonging to the Trustees. He wrote, " . . . it seems to me unnecessary and improper (as it will no doubt, I think, do, to the

Honourable Committee, when they have learnt the nature of these circumstances) to trouble His Grace, the Archbishop of York, in reference to the subject. For the same reasons, it would be advisable also, as far as I can see, not to have recourse to the Patron, since, owing to a great peculiarity of circumstances, in the construction of the Deeds by which the Church Lands, here, are held, the Patron has nothing whatever to do with them—I have, however, procured the formal consent of the major part of the Trustees, and herewith send it" (2). The Parsonage was apparently built on similar authority.

Though the Trustees were responsible for the maintenance of "a preaching minister" it would appear that they did not assume the responsibility of providing a residence until the first Parsonage was built in 1778. Such records as are available suggest that the parson had hitherto lived in his own house. The first reference to a parsonage is in Haworth Parish Register. On the 15th May 1739 "at 6 o'clock in the Evening, the Houses in Haworth called the Parsonage, were solemnly Dedicated, and so named, with Prayers, Aspersions, Acclamations and Crossings" by Isaac Smith the then incumbent. These houses must have been his own, because three months later he did fealty at the Manor Court for "the Houses called the Parsonage late the property of James Moone of Haworth". It has sometimes been assumed that these Houses were at Sowdens where Mr. Grimshaw lived, but neither the Parish Register nor the Court Rolls give any indication of their location, and Sowdens was then the property of John Fields. In 1733 James Moone mortgaged his property on the Green to Isaac Smith to secure £150, but remained in occupation for some time at least. Moone held various properties in Haworth and was selling between 1734 and 1739. The Register and Court Rolls indicate that there was a good deal of mortgaging, buying and selling of land taking place during the period, probably due to the break up of the Emmott estate.

The Reverend Isaac Smith died in 1742 and was succeeded by the Reverend William Grimshaw, who, in November 1742 purchased from John Fields of Shipley "a messuage with appurtenances called Sowdens wherein James Taylor did formerly dwell" (3) and at the next Manor Court (which was not held until 1748) he did fealty "for Sowdens". It appears from the deeds enrolled at the Wakefield Registry that this property was originally purchased by Christopher and Bryan Sowden from the lord of the manor and

(2) B.S.T. vol. 16 p.351
(3) Wakefield Registry of deeds p.704 p.1031

passed from them to James Taylor who sold it to John Fields in 1738. In his replies to questions asked before the Visitation of Archbishop Herring in June 1743, Grimshaw states "I do reside personally upon my cure, not in a Parsonage House, for I have none, I reside notwithstanding commodiously for the observance of my duty in the parish and near the Church" (4). Several references in the deeds at Wakefield Registry confirm Grimshaw's ownership of Sowdens. The Parish Register records that "Rev. William Grimshaw died April 7th 1763 at Sowdens" and in his Will dated 24th March 1763 he left Sowdens to his son, John, on condition that John paid various outstanding debts.

The residences of his successor, the Reverend John Richardson, are more difficult to trace. There was a delay in his taking office due to a temporary disagreement between the Trustees and the Vicar of Bradford and, though he signed the marriage register once in September 1763, he was not licensed by the Archbishop until September 1764. Replying to questions put before Archbishop Drummond's Visitation in February 1764 he said "I do not reside personally upon my cure but at Huddersfield. It has hitherto been inconvenient to reside at Haworth. I have a residing curate, Mr. Bliss . . . *there is no parsonage house*, he boards in the parish and has the whole income of the place". In 1771 John Richardson did fealty in the manor court for "a farm at Marsh End purchased from Roger Metcalfe". There is no evidence that he ever lived there, but it remained in his possession until his death in 1791 when Marsh End was left in his Will to his nephew Joseph Richardson. In the court rolls he is described as "of Sowden" in 1775. Horsfall Turner states Richardson lived at "Cook House" but gives no authority.

About this time the Trustees, no doubt aware of the inconvenience of having no permanent residence for the parson, and as funds were accumulating, decided to embark on the building of a parsonage. In 1774 John Wright, a yeoman of Haworth who farmed land in Haworth near the church, agreed to sell to Richard Townend, a piece-maker of Haworth, some land called the Croft on the north side of the present Church Street, containing "two days work" (an area of about one acre) and sixteen roods for £840. Before the sale was effected, however, the Church Trustees "having a sum of money in their hands given by the donations of different persons for the use of the parochial chapel" had contracted with Richard

(4) Yorkshire Archaeological Society. Record Series 72 p.39

Townend to purchase part of the land (later called Parson's Croft and being the area known as two days work) for £137. The conveyance was completed by a deed known as Lease and Release dated the 9th and 10th September 1774. A receipt for £137 is endorsed on the Release and the Trustees did fealty for the land at the next manor court.

This deed stated that it was the intention of the Trustees to use the profits of the land "towards the maintenance of a preaching minister". It also empowered them "by sale mortage or otherwise" to raise a sum of money on the premises for building a dwelling-house "upon the said premises *or elsewhere*" for the use of the minister, and they obviously took up the option to build elsewhere, for the Parsonage was, in fact, built in 1778 on a site called Halsteads opposite the Croft on the other side of what is now called Church Street. The sexton's cottage, the National School, and the Church Sunday School were later to be built on the Croft.

The Terrier

The Terrier (5) of 1781 (Plate 2) describes the Croft as "a close of land called The Croft now in possession of the Curate containing two days work or upwards which has lately been purchased by the Trustees of the Chapel of Haworth for £137, part of the sum of £195 given by Christopher and John Scott for the Curates of Haworth to have the interest therefrom . . . £58 being the residue of the sum of £195 is laid out by the Trustees on building a barn which standeth in the aforesaid close called The Croft. It is built with stone and is covered with slate being 13 yards in length and 9 yards in breadth being in possession of the Curate". In successive terriers and deeds this one acre and barn, having been acquired with money left for he Curates, are always said to belong to the chapel and to bet occupied by the Curate. During some part of Mr. Brontë's time, however, other arrangements must have been made, because in a deed of 1854 John Feather was named as tenant of the Parson's Croft and barn, while Mr. Brontë is described as tenant of only the "Parsonage house, buildings and garden". This deed was executed to appoint new Trustees "by reason that Patrick Brontë was far advanced in life . . . for enabling the new appointed Trustees to vote in the nomination of a Parson . . . when a vacancy took place". In the Reverend John Wade's time the Croft and barn reverted to

(5) Document recording site, boundaries, property etc.

A true Note and Terrier of all the Glebe Lands Meadows and other Rights &

Imprimis

Curate of the said Chapel

the Chapel Yard containing one Rood and Twenty perches adjoining to the Town of
hereinafter particularly described part whereof were given by Mess: Christopher Scott and John Scott and

One Farm or Tenement now in the Tenure or Occupation of James Wignal the House is built with Stone and co
with Slate being sixteen Yards in Length and six in Breadth with Twelve Closes of Land thereto belongi
Hollings on the West to the Lands of Mr Joseph Pollard on the North to the Turnpike Road leading f
of Keighley and now let at the clear yearly Rent of Twenty five pounds and ten Shillings And anoth
with Slate being Twelve Yards in Length and six in Breadth and the Barn is built with Stone and cove
Twelve Acres one Rood and Twenty three perches Adjoining on the East to the Lands of George Taylor on
Stanbury and on the South to the said Brook which divides the said Township of Haworth from th
Tenement now in the Tenure or Occupation of Christopher Holmes the House is built with Stone a
is built with Stone and covered with Slate being Twelve Yards in Length and six in Breadth with
East and South to the Lands of the said George Taylor on the West to the Lands now occupied by the
of Nine pounds one Shilling and six pence And another Farm or Tenement now in the Tenure or
Length and six in Breadth with one Cottage built with Stone and covered with Slate b
being Twelve Yards in Length and six in Breadth with Six Closes of Land thereto belonging
East West North and South of the Lands of the said James Wignal And another part thereof
yearly Rent of ~~fifteen Pounds~~ and ten Shillings And another Farm or Tenement now in t
Seven Yards in Length and five in Breadth and the Barn is built with Stone and covered w
containing eleven Acres one Rood and eighteen perches Adjoining on the East to the Lands
of Inheritance on the North to the Lands of the said Joseph Pollard and on the South to sai
at the clear yearly Rent of Twelve pounds and eighteen Shillings Also one Close of Land called
been purchased by the Trustees of the said Chapel of Haworth for the sum of one Hundred a
said Christopher Scott and John Scott for the Curates of Haworth aforesaid to have the Interest
of York Gentleman and the Sum of Fifty eight pounds being the Residue of the said Sum of One Hund
standeth in the aforesaid Close of Ground called the Croft it is built with Stone and covered with Sla
Benefit belonging to the said Chapel consists in the Surplice Dues And there is in the Steeple th
of Administering the holy Sacrament And Two Pewter Flaggons the one hath this Inscripti
Mercy bestows And all from his passion our Happiness flows A D 1750 And the other ha
Redeeming Grace or Dying Love 1756 There is a Silver Chalice with these Letters upon it H I
The Inhabitants are charged with the Repairs of the Edifices and Chapel Yard fence The Clerk is paid that
of his Wages are what the Inhabitants are pleased to bestow upon him when he goes about annually
Wages for every Grave making and tolling the Bell In Testimony of the truth of the beforemention
Haworth aforesaid have hereunto set our Hands the 27th — Day of June One Thousand Seve

14   Plate 2.   Terrier of 1781.

the parochial Chapel of Haworth in the Diocese of York now in the use and possession of the Revd John Richardson

on the South and to the Lands of Richard Emmott Esquire on the East West and North Also the Farms
purchased All of them situate lying and being at Stanbury in the Township of Haworth aforesaid

Slate being Twenty yards in Length and six in Breadth And the Barn is built with Stone and covered
ing Twenty two Acres and Twelve Perches of Statute Measure adjoining on the East to the Lands of Joseph
lord to Coln and on the South to the Brook which divides the said Township of Haworth from the parish
or Tenement now in the Tenure or Occupation of Widow Townend the House is built with Stone and covered
to being eight yards in Length and six in Breadth with five Closes of Land thereto belonging containing
to the Lands of Michael Cousin on the North to the Brook which divides the Hamlet of Haworth and
ish of Keighley And is now let at the clear yearly Rent of Thirteen pounds And another Farm or
d with Slate being Twelve yards in Length and five and an Half in Breadth and the Barn
of Land thereto belonging containing Eleven Acres two Roods and thirty Perches Adjoining on the
ow Townend and on the North to the Lands of Mr Wilson and is now let at the clear yearly Rent
of James Robinson the House is built with Stone and covered with Slate being Nine yards in
ards in Length and three in Breadth and one Barn built with Stone and covered with Slate
g Eleven Acres two Roods and thirty Perches One part of the said Lands is Adjoining to the
ing to the East and West on the Lands of the said Joseph Hollings And now let at the clear
or Occupation of Isaac Willman the House is built with Stone and covered with Slate being
ing Twelve yards in Length and Six in Breadth with four Closes of Land thereto belonging
Tenure or Occupation of James Wignal on the West to the said James Wignals own Lands
which divides the said Township of Haworth from the said parish of Keighley And now let
now in the possession of the said Curate containing two Days Work or Upwards which has lately
seven Pounds being part of the sum of One Hundred and Ninety five pounds given by the
refrom and which was lately let out at Interest to Joseph Hollings of Cottingley in the said County
ty five pounds is laid out by the Trustees of the Chapel of Haworth in building a Barn which
teen Yards in Length and Nine in Breadth being in possession of the Curate And the rest of the
and a Clock and in the Chancel a Communion Table with a Linnen Cloth to cover it at the time
Jesus we live in Jesus we rest And thankful receive his dying Bequest The Cup of Salvation his
st Jesus what delicious Fare How Sweet thine Entertainments are Near did Angels taste above
Books belonging to the Chapel are a Bible two Common prayer Books and a Book of Homilies
out of the Church Rates for Wages for cleaning the Church and other things relating thereto And the Rest
he same Also the Sexton is paid by the Inhabitants the sum of one Shilling and two pence for his
s and every of them We the Minister Churchwardens and principal Inhabitants of
and Eighty One

John Richardson
Curate of Haworth

Robert Feather } Church
John Booth } Warden

Michael Cousin
Stephen Beaver
Jno Roberts
John Murgatroyd

his use (6). The barn was demolished in 1903 when the new Sunday School was built, and in 1960 the Charity Commissioners gave permission for the sale of "0.8 acres known as Parson's Croft with the building thereon used as a Sunday School". The Sunday School was then demolished and a car-park now occupies the site.

Halsteads

Four years after the purchase of The Croft, the Trustees bought from Richard Emmott the land known as *Halsteads* on which the first Parsonage was built. It was conveyed by a deed of Lease and Release dated the 17th and 18th August 1778. The Emmotts were large landowners in Haworth and one branch of the family resided for many years at the Old Hall. Richard Emmott had left Haworth, and at the time of the sale was living in Goldens (Goldings) in Hertfordshire. The land was described as "seven hundred and eighty square yards whereon a dwellinghouse and other conveniences are *now erecting* taken off and from a certain close called Halsteads situate near the Church at Haworth upon the West now in possession of James Wood with . . . one way to be made use of from the dwelling house now erecting leading from the town of Haworth between a house belonging to John Greenwood' and the church called Church Lane". This is the same plot of land "with Rectory and outbuild-ings" sold to the Brontë Society in 1928 for £3000, the gift of Sir James Roberts. Richard Emmott's lands were surveyed in 1769 (plate 2) and, though the original survey cannot now be found, a photographic copy of the survey and plan relating to his lands in Haworth is in the Library. This is the earliest plan of the district we have. All the fields numbered 4 in the plan were in the tenancy of James Wood of the "Bull Inn" according to the survey, including Halsteads. The field next to it is called Kirk Hill, but a later plan shows Kirk Hill incorporated with the fields there designated Higher and Lower Halsteads and the Parsonage built on the enclosure taken from Higher Halsteads, in the corner of what, in 1769, was called Kirk Hill. This incorporation took place before 1778, when the land bought by the Trustees was described as being taken from Halsteads. About this time, Richard Emmott was selling much of his Haworth lands which were being renamed.

It is interesting to note that at the time of Emmott's survey James Wood was also a tenant of eight perches of land called "Church

16

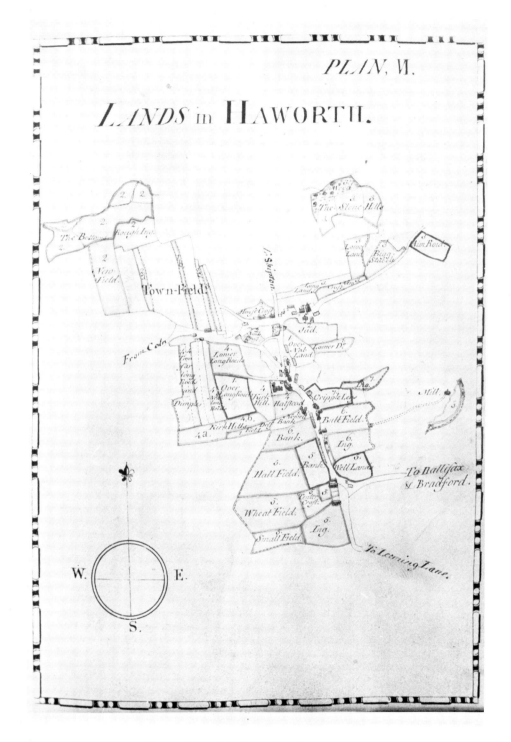

Plate 3. Plan of Richard Emmott's Lands in Haworth, 1769.

Lane". At this period Church Street did not extend as far as the Parsonage and a way to the new dwellinghouse was reserved in the 1778 deed.

Date of Building

There is no record of the date when the building was finished nor when John Richardson moved into the new Parsonage. From the deed of 1778 it is clear that by August of that year the Parsonage was in course of erection and it would probably be completed before the end of the year. It has often been stated that the glebe house was fit for residence in 1779, but without valid evidence. Writing in 1879 Horsfall Turner lists (7) the information relating to Haworth as given by George Lawton in 1840 (8). The entry that "the Glebe House is fit for residence" follows an entry dated 1779 relating to the erection of a gallery in the Church. Lawton, however, in his Preface states that his information relating to glebe houses was taken from the "Returns to the Church Revenue Commissioners". Nowhere in the volume does he give a date for these Returns, but evidently they were taken from the completed Articles of Enquiry sent to incumbents by the Ecclesiastical Revenues Commission Office in 1832. Article 13 asks the incumbent to state "whether there is a Glebe House fit for residence of the Incumbent, and if unfit, why?". Mr. Brontë replied, "There is a house commonly occupied by the incumbent—which house is not rightly affixed to the perpetual curacy but is under the control of trustees". John Richardson, the first curate to occupy the Parsonage, died in 1791 and had probably lived there for about eleven years, but it is a coincidence that his occupation began about the same time as a new gallery was erected in the Church. The Reverend James Charnock lived at the Parsonage for another twenty-eight years, but no written records are available of any alterations made to the original building until Mr. Brontë's time. Mr. Brontë's reply to the Revenue Commissioners quoted above states "a house *commonly* occupied by the incumbent". This implies that at some time the house may have been occupied by someone else. Certainly there is a suspicion that Mr. Charnock was not living in the house 1813/14.

(7) Haworth Past and Present p.23
(8) Collectio Rerum Ecclesiasticarum de Diocesi Eboracensi 1840

17

Haworth January 1st 1797.

An Account of Money receiv'd & paid by Robert Heaton
Church Warden —

	L.	s.	D.
Allowed for Expences	0	1	6
Feby 7th Paid the Expences of Measuring the Enlargement of the church yard, and the Letting the Walling of the same, and getting and leading the Stones	0	13	0
March 16th Paid for an Almanac			6
Ditto. Paid Jonathan Utley for new hinging 1 Bell		16	6
— 20 paid for Footing Church yard Wall			5
Do — cutting part of the ground work		1	6
April 1st paid Jonathan Whalley for Do		2	—
— 11 gave Masons for Drink			1
— 17 Paid Joseph Foster			10
Do Paid Bradford Church Wardens		10	
Expences		1	6
May 1st Paid Henry Atkinson for Foster's Cloaths	2	6	6
— for 1lb of Candles			10
12 Paid John Jowett for a Stone		3	6
paid Henry Holmes for Stones for Church Yard		5	3
15 paid Masons for Walling the Church Yard	24	9	—
J. Judson for measuring Do		2	—
for Lime for ch: yard Wall	4	9	4
for pulling up, and removing part of the Church Yard Wall and dressing Stones off the field after Masons		17	2
Paid Joseph Speak for Leading Stones, Sand &c for Do	5	13	—
June 16th Paid Expences at Visitation		1	10
for Letting Ground work of North Side of ch: Yard Wall, pulling up the Wall at East end & leveling the ch: yard, and causeway	2	10	—
for Court Fees & — for Horse Hire 2. which makes		11	—
Augst 1st Paid for Foster's Cloaths making		6	—
Paid Joseph Speak's Bill for 1796 including Easter 1797	1	18	—
for Hingings to J. Moor		10	11
Septr 4th Paid Abilly Hey Interest for 50	2	5	—
Dr 11 Paid Joseph Wright his Interest		9	—
Allowed for Collecting Church Leys			
	L 75	10	9

The Plot and Garden

The Trustees, having obtained the land from Richard Emmott, began to build the Parsonage in 1778. We have no evidence that there was any building already on the site, but the possibility should not be overlooked. The house was built well back on the site in order to give a reasonably large garden at the front (plate 1). Facing east, it benefits from the morning sun, an important factor in the days when artificial light was both poor and expensive—in the 18th century people rose early and went to bed at dark. The parsonage, as is the case of many rectories and vicarages, has a churchyard on the east and south. When Mr. Brontë arrived in 1819 this had already been extended. The church wardens' accounts (plate 4) show that Robert Heaton (a trustee) received and paid in February 1797 13/-d for "measuring the enlargements of the churchyard" and later, Thomas Sugden was paid £3 for pulling down the wall on the north side and building a new one (9). Nevertheless, the churchyard was beginning to approach the garden wall and in 1821 more land, to extend it further on the south-west side, was bought from Thomas Brooksbank Charnock, the son of Mr. Brontë's predecessor. Mrs. Gaskell describes the house as being "surrounded on three sides by the churchyard". This was not true then and indeed, is not true today. When the Brontës first came to Haworth the churchyard lay only on the east side, and to the south and west were open fields. On the north the small piece of accommodation land which provided access to the Parsonage and the barn, divided the garden from the Croft. The barn, which was not occupied by the Brontës, was pulled down in 1903. (right of plate 5). The approach to the house was up the short lane now called Church Street, and a gate in the front garden wall, opening on to the churchyard, was used by Mr. Brontë on his way to and from the Church. Exactly where this gate was situated is uncertain, but it is unlikely to have been where the "Gate of the Dead" (never so called by the Brontës) now stands, since this would have involved walking over the graves, which Mr. Brontë would never have done. The *Bradford Review* account of Mr. Brontë's funeral states, "The corpse was brought out

Plate 5.   View showing the barn demolished in 1903.

through the eastern gate of the garden leading to the churchyard''. There is a suggestion that the gate was nearer the corner of the garden.

Mrs. Gaskell, describing the Parsonage, writes there was a "small grass enclosure for drying clothes" at the rear, but it seems this was not large enough, for in Mr. Brontë's notebook we find he paid John Brown (the tenant) 2/-d a year "for leave to hang up the clothes for drying in his field". In 1848 he paid William Wood 2/2d for a "close pole" (clothes pole). The house in the Brontës' time did not extend to the curtilage as it now does and so one could walk all round it.

An old photograph seems to show a substantial single storey lean-to building with stone flagged roof against the north wall of the house. This could have been for storing garden tools or household fuel, it existed in the late 19th century, but when it was built is not known.

The accommodation land on the north side of the house has had various names—Kirk Hill—Parsonage Lane—Church Lane— and is now classified as Church Street. An interesting feature of the plan in the possession of Mr. Arthur Hartley (plate 6) is a footpath shown

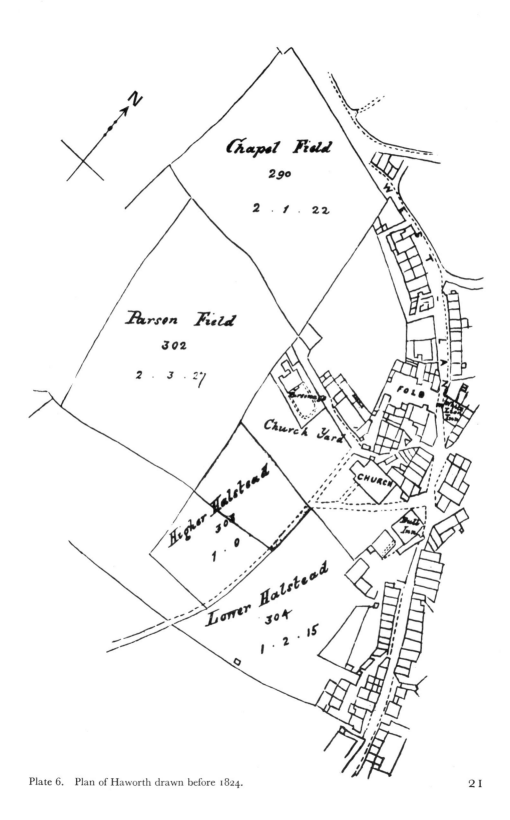

N

Chapel Field
290
2 . 1 . 22

Parson Field
302
2 . 3 . 27

WEST LANE

FOLD

BLACK
Bull
Inn

Browes

Church Yard

CHURCH

Higher Halstead
303
1 . 0

Bull
Inn

Lower Halstead
304
1 . 2 . 15

Plate 6.   Plan of Haworth drawn before 1824.

circling the garden, and this also appears on the Tithe Award map of 1849. Mr. Brontë's notebook has an entry "I will never flag the garden walks . . . it would cost £5, look worse, be more slippery in frost - require washing, & produce weeds between the joinings" (10).

Old photographs show the garden sheltered from the prevailing wind by a belt of bushes and low trees, among these were mountain ashes and hawthorns; the tall pine trees were not planted until 1854. There was a lawn in front of the house and flower beds at the side. Mr. James M. Hoppin, on a visit to the Parsonage after Charlotte's death, was taken by Mr. Nicholls "through a high walled yard at the back of the house around to the front through a small flower garden". Other visitors state that the Parsonage was well screened at both front and rear by a high wall and that little could be seen except the kitchen window. Emily was the 'head gardener' and was much obliged for the flower seeds sent by Ellen Nussey of Sicilian pea and crimson cornflowers, and enquired whether or not they required a sheltered spot. In her Diary Paper of July 30th 1845 she writes "Anne and I should have picked the blackcurrants if the weather had been fine and sunshiny". The garden contained a variety of fruit bushes.

The whole property was surrounded by a stone wall and a gate in the wall at the top of Church Lane gave access to the back door. This high wall, altered in Mr. Wade's time, protected the privacy of the inhabitants: neither Charlotte nor Mr. Brontë liked "gazers".

(10) B.S.T. vol. 14, part 72 p.19

The Parsonage House

Design

The front of Haworth Parsonage has been sketched and photographed so many times that a general description is unnecessary. Plans and drawings of what remains of the original home should be examined by those requiring architectural information. Unfortunately no pictorial evidence of the rear of the house has so far been found and only evidence based on later plans and Brontë letters is available (plates 7 and 8).

The original house remains substantially as it was built, the gable wing being added after the time of the Brontës on the north side (plate 1). The Parsonage has been depicted by many writers, following in Mrs. Gaskell's footsteps, as a gloomy house though to many visitors it appears, to their surprise, a delightful home of good proportions lit by elegant sash windows. The front elevation has a pleasing simplicity which reflects great credit on the unknown builder. The size and symmetrical placing of the windows and the pedimented doorway, bear a happy relationship to the wall space, the whole drawn together by the roof line with two well-designed chimney stacks. The effect is one of substantial comfort with a touch of refinement in the workmanship.

The design is a typical late Georgian rectangular house (plate 12) with a doorway in the centre, a room with two windows on each side and bedrooms of equivalent size above; the centre window above the front door lights a small room over the hall. The large gabled wing on the north side was added by the Rev. John Wade (Mr. Brontë's successor) in 1878 to plans drawn by Messrs. Milnes & France in 1872 (plate 7). Having been built long after the Brontës were dead, this wing need not concern us in detail. Apparently the house was in need of repair when Mr. Wade took over and Mr. Nicholls, writing from Ireland where he had gone when Mr. Brontë died in November 1861, said, "There are extensive alterations going on at the Parsonage I understand, I dare say I shall not know it when I see it". One of Mr. Wade's changes was to remove the

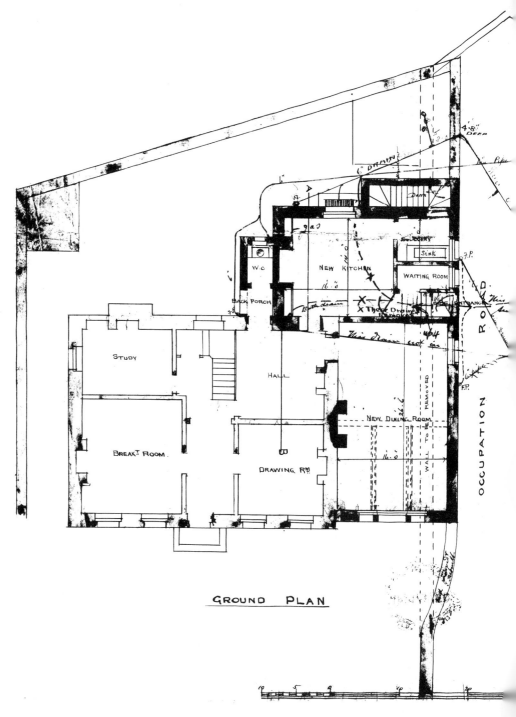

Labels within the plan:
W.C.

NEW KITCHEN

BACK PORCH

STUDY

HALL

BREAK^T ROOM

DRAWING R^M

Sink

WAITING ROOM

NEW DINING ROOM

OCCUPATION ROAD

GROUND PLAN

Plate 7.   Plan of Rev. John Wade's alterations, drawn 1872.

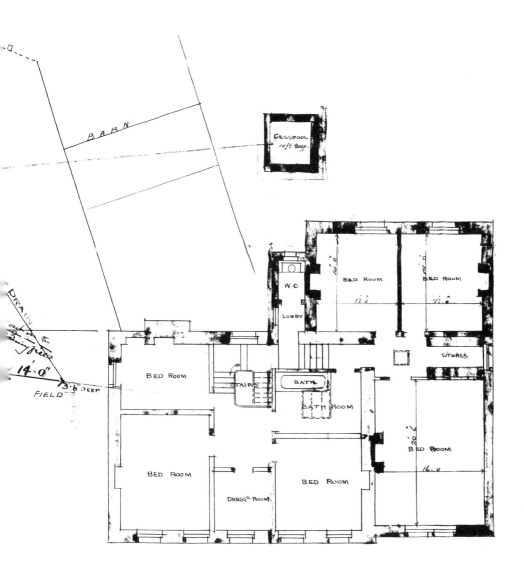

BARN

CESSPOOL
10ft Deep.

DRAIN
out in the
field

14'0"

3'6 DEEP

FIELD

BED ROOM

STAIRS

W.C

LOBBY

BATH

BATH ROOM

BED ROOM.
12.0
14'0"

BED ROOM
12'0"
14'0"

STORES

BED ROOM.
16.0
20'6"

BED ROOM

BED ROOM

DRESS⁰ ROOM

CHAMBER PLAN

40   50   60   70

25

small Georgian window panes and put in plate glass. This had been completed by 1866 according to Emma Cortazzo, a friend of Ellen Nussey (11). This gave the house a 'contemporary' look but destroyed the eighteenth century atmosphere at a stroke. In 1955 the house was transformed by the re-instatement of glazing bars to the windows and this did more than anything else to restore the original appearance.

The hall, store room and kitchen floors are stone, covered with Elland flags and in the time of the Brontës these were sanded according to Mrs. Gaskell. The custom of rubbing the flags with a wet sand-stone (scouring stone) around the floor near the walls was widely practised in the North of England. Sometimes a pattern was drawn in the wet sand with the fingers, showing up when the sanding had dried to a white or yellow colour. This embellishment would be carried out every few days and no-one would dare set foot on it.

In Mr. Wade's time, the ground floor level was raised by about 5 inches by laying a wooden floor over the existing flags in the study and dining room as this made the rooms warmer. However, this necessitated raising all the other flagged floors to the same level. The raising of the hall floor meant that the front door was too large so it was reduced in height by altering the top panel, which accounts for its unusual proportions. The style and construction indicate that this door could well be the one inserted when the house was built in 1778.

The raising of the floor level allowed air grates to be put in, suggesting Mr. Wade perhaps found dry rot in the building. A report in the *Bronte Society Transactions* of 1955 mentions that the front steps had subsided 3 inches and had to be raised; it seems the steps were settling back to their original level. The level of the yard at the rear has been raised by about 1½ft. since the house was built, for doorways previously opening from the outside to Mr. Nicholls' study are now sunk at the base below the flags of the yard. A survey by the architects Kitson, Parish & Ledgard in 1928 advised laying a concrete floor in the dining room as a fire precaution. Similar treatment was given to the ceiling and the door was reinforced with steel sheeting as a further precaution.

An interesting account appears in the *Bronte Society Transactions* (12) of a visit to Haworth by Mr. Charles Hale in 1861 in which he says "The house is a hundred years old and is sadly out of repair, for Mr. Brontë disliked to have mechanical work going on there. Only

(11) B.S.T. vol. 13 p.222
(12) B.S.T. vol. 15 p.134-5

once out of necessity to keep out bad leakage he allowed the roof to be mended. The new incumbent does not choose to go into a rotten old house, but they are doing very much more than making merely necessary repairs. They are putting in fireplaces and mantel pieces of marble and windows of plate glass, a single pane filling the whole sash and weighing 30 pounds. The stone walls, stone floors of the passages, and stone staircase, will stand unchanged for another hundred years as they have the last, but the masonry is new pointed and the house will be refitted anew throughout. In old Tabby's chamber, for some reason, half the window had been walled up with a stone wall by Mr. Brontë's direction; this erection has been pulled down . . . I purchased the whole lower sash of the window of the bedroom of Charlotte Brontë. This is the window at which she was most fond of sitting . . . I also brought away plenty of the moulding or woodwork that went about the rooms so I can frame photographs".

An article in *Chambers Journal* entitled "A Winter Day at Haworth" describes "the humble dwelling" under the leaden sky at the top of "the long unlovely street" and adds, no doubt because of the long high wall, that without being impertinent it was only possible to see "the roof and window of the kitchen where the three sisters used to help Tabby with the household work". The rear of the house was still untouched but plate glass had been inserted into the windows.

Mr. Wade swept away many of the internal features of the Parsonage in order to modernise it. Before condemning his action it should be compared with the wholesale modernisation taking place in old houses today. Mr. Wade did not alter the window frames, only the glazing, he left the original doors and he put the house in good repair. It might have been less fortunate. His addition of the north wing meant breaking through a doorway from the old kitchen to his *new* dining room and, in addition, he extended behind the house. The existing kitchen arrangements were old-fashioned and not sufficient for his requirements, so the domestic offices were extended by building a larger kitchen wing behind the house with bedrooms above. This blocked up both the kitchen window and that of the room above, both these rooms becoming virtually passages to the new north wing. It is possible that Mr. Brontë himself had built a lean-to extension to the kitchen in later life, probably in the late 1840's or in 1851. However, no evidence to substantiate this

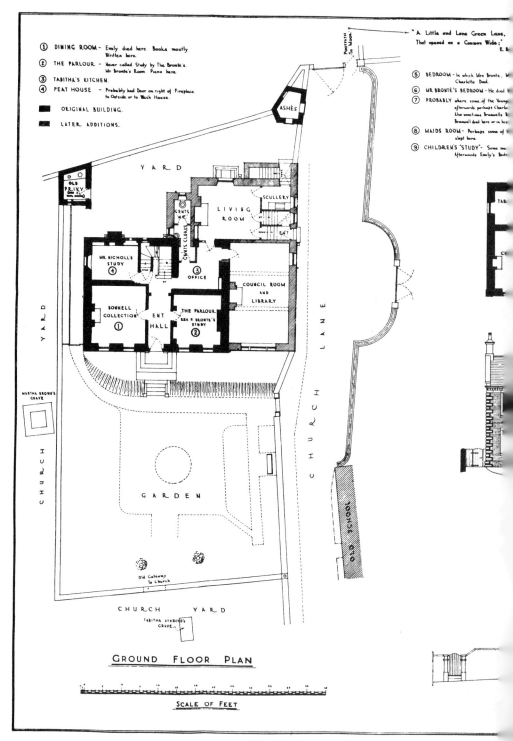

① **DINING ROOM** – Emily died here. Books mostly Written here.

② **THE PARLOUR** – Never called Study by The Bronte's. Mr Bronte's Room. Piano here.

③ **TABITHA'S KITCHEN.**

④ **PEAT HOUSE** – Probably had Door on right of Fireplace to Outside or to Wash House.

▓ **ORIGINAL BUILDING.**

▓ **LATER ADDITIONS.**

⑤ **BEDROOM** – In which Mrs Bronte, M___ Charlotte Died.

⑥ **MR BRONTE'S BEDROOM** – He died i___

⑦ **PROBABLY** where some of the Young___ afterwards perhaps Charlo___ Also sometimes Branwell h___ Branwell died here or in his

⑧ **MAIDS ROOM** – Perhaps some of t___ slept here.

⑨ **CHILDREN'S "STUDY"** – Some ma___ Afterwards Emily's Bed___

"A Little and Lone Green Lane,
That opened on a Common Wide;"
E. B___

YARD

OLD PRIVY

GENTS W.C.

GENTS CLOAKS

SCULLERY

LIVING ROOM

MR NICHOLL'S STUDY ④

OFFICE ③

COUNCIL ROOM AND LIBRARY

BONNELL COLLECTION ①

ENT HALL

THE PARLOUR REV. P. BRONTE'S STUDY ②

ASHES

FOOTPATH To Moor

CHURCH LANE

OLD SCHOOL

YARD

MARTHA BROWN'S GRAVE

GARDEN

Old Gateway To Church

CHURCH YARD

TABITHA AYKROYD'S GRAVE

GROUND FLOOR PLAN

SCALE OF FEET

Plate 8. Plan of the Parsonage, 1936.

Brontë Parsonage Museum
Haworth

ST FLOOR PLAN

BASEMENT PLAN

NT ELEVATION

BACK ELEVATION

ON TO CHURCH LANE

ELEVATION TO CHURCH YARD

FRED MITCHELL & SONS F & A.I.A.A.
ARCHITECTS & SURVEYORS.
9 UPPER FOUNTAINS STREET,
ALBION STREET   LEEDS.
APRIL   1936.

29

Plate 9. Architect's sketch of 1957 extensions.

has come to light. The photograph on plate 14 was taken after 1859 and does not show the extension clearly, but it appears that either the extension was large, or that it is the original old block joined by the passage. Certainly, if Mr. Brontë built anything at the rear, it must have been behind the kitchen as the rest of the rear wall shows no sign of having been altered. Unfortunately, subsequent alterations cover up the outside wall of the Brontë's kitchen, obliterating any evidence for this suggestion.

Layout of the House

For the guidance of readers, plans of the Parsonage have been included and can be found on plates 6, 7 and 8. Though only a block plan (plate 6) of the original house can be found, it is of interest in that it shows the outline of the property. In the original Deed of Purchase of 1778 the land is shown as 780 square yards. This same figure recurs throughout the later deeds relating to the property in 1778, 1823, 1854, 1872, 1928 and 1957. The earlier plan (plate 6) is in the possession of Mr. Arthur Hartley of Haworth and can be dated by the presence, or absence, of other properties shown. For example, the barn at the corner of the Croft was built by the Trustees in, or soon after 1774, and this barn appears on the plan. In 1824 the entrance to St. Michael's Church was altered, and the steps and gates built at the time exist today, but these do not appear. We can, therefore, deduce that the plan was drawn before 1824. The 1778 deed says "a dwelling house and *other conveniences* are now erecting". The other conveniences must have been out-buildings. The barn was not part of the Parsonage property, being situated on the Croft, not on Halsteads. When new Trustees were appointed in 1845 the deed stated that Mr. Brontë was the tenant of "the Parsonage house, *buildings* and garden". He was not a tenant of the Croft or the barn which were occupied by John Feather. The 1849 Enclosure Award confirms this, as does the deed of 1854 and the plan on plate 6 shows that there were originally more buildings attached to the Parsonage than previously thought. The map accompanying the Tithe Award of 1849 shows a similar outline of the buildings. The unusual arrangement of a building standing at a distance from the main body of the house and joining it by a passageway, suggests that it was added later to provide further accommodation. An alternative suggestion is that this ex-tension was a building much older than the Parsonage which was utilised when the house was built in 1778. Such an arrangement of buildings joined by a passage allows both blocks to have windows on all four sides. Ellen Nussey's account of the Parsonage has an inter-esting bearing on the stone mullioned window in the room above Mr. Nicholl's study described as Tabitha's room (13). She wrote that "the room at the back on the right as you mount the staircase was a small room allotted to Branwell as a studio, the *one room in the house* with an open view to the moors above Stanbury and the Sladen Valley". There are two significant points here, the first that the window must have been blocked up by the Brontës and not by a previous tenant of the Parsonage. Secondly, it confirms the exis-tence at the time of a high building to the rear of the house, for had there been no such building the same view would have been obtained from the room across the landing. As things stood, the domestic wing at the rear obstructed any such view.

The plan (plate 6) shows a small square on the south-west corner of the main building. This was an outside staircase to Tabitha's room which was at one time inaccessible from inside the house. Both the outside and inside wall of Tabitha's room at this point show evidence of a doorway in the wall giving access to this staircase.

The early plan (plate 6) in conjunction with the plan for Mr. Wade's alterations (plate 7) however, confirms the previous existence of a back kitchen. On Mr. Wade's plan the old drainage system appears in dotted lines. By plotting these drains on to the plan on plate 6 it can be seen that they run from two points, joining near the curtilage, and running downhill across the lane to a soakaway in the Croft (not the cesspool on the Wade plan). One drain starts at a point in the kitchen in the Parsonage between the window and the little door to the new office built in 1958 at a point where the pump was sited. The other drain starts near the north west corner of the block at the rear, probably to drain a sink in the back kitchen. "Sally Mosley is washing in the back kitchin". This back kitchen may have been the main *working* kitchen of the house. Charlotte wrote to Emily October 1st 1843, "I should like uncommonly to be in the dining room at home, or in the kitchen, or in the *back kitchen* . . . cutting up the hash".

At the north corner of the back yard another small building (plate 6) is also marked; a single storey building, standing against the high wall which ran up the lane, and was probably the one known as the "peat house" by the Brontës. In a house run by someone as fastidious as Aunt Branwell who did not greatly favour the family pets, it would seem more reasonable that the pet geese were housed here, not in a room behind the dining room. Mrs. Gaskell refers to this room, which became Mr. Nicholls' study, as "a sort of flagged store-room" and makes no mention of peat or geese. The dotted lines in the front garden on plate 6 depict the garden path. In the north-west corner of the 1936 plan (plate 8) there is a small building marked "Ashes". This is not the old peat house, but a building put up during Mr. Wade's time, on land bought when he made the extension. The old peat house can just be seen within the original 1778 curtilage, marked in the top north-west corner on the 1872 plan (plate 7). It had been demolished by 1936 and so does not appear on the 1936 plan (plate 8). The building on the south wall was the privy which was demolished in 1958 as it was by then beyond repair.

The passageway which joined the house to the back kitchen could well be the one that the dying Emily used when going to the back kitchen to collect food for her dogs and "when she reached the flagged passage the cold took her". This passage gave access to the back door which was approached from the lane by a short flight of steps from a gate in the high wall at a point just beyond the north-west corner of the house. This wall originally ran the full length of the north boundary of the property, and Mr. Wade's extension involved its removal in the vicinity of the house. Originally, the Trustees owned this part of Church Street and so were thus able to extend into it. This change is clearly visible from the road today. In the Brontës' time the old flagged footpath only extended up Parsonage Lane, now called Church Street, as far as the back entrance to the old part of the house. The curve in the footpath shows the change of line from the old path to the 1878 line.

The double dotted line intersecting the plan of the Wade extension (plate 7) marked "wall to be removed" shows the old boundary of the garden as it was in the time of the Brontës. The wall thicknesses on the 1872 and 1936 plans of the rooms (plates 7 and 8) are not accurately drawn and the 'to scale' drawing on plate 13 shows the discrepancies. The 1872 plan (plate 7) shows the wall and doorway in Charlotte's bedroom in its original place; it seems the architect could have been working from original plans, and did not trouble to bring up to date the plan of the existing part of the house which was not being altered.

Restoring the Home

Plate 8 shows a plan of the Parsonage drawn in 1936 for publication in the *Transactions*. In 1956 the Council of the Brontë Society felt that the time had come to improve facilities at the Museum, as the living quarters of the custodian, who at that time was accommodated in the Parsonage, left much to be desired. More space was needed for the exhibition of documents, pictures and other items, and an added problem was the increasing number of visitors passing up and down the only staircase. The Council, therefore, decided that they must take action. Plans were drawn up by Messrs. Jones & Stocks of Leeds in 1957 and more land to the south and west purchased. A flat for the custodian was designed as a separate entity, joined by a wide covered way to the Museum (plate 9). The opportunity was taken to restore the Parsonage as near as possible to the home it was in the Brontës' time. In the past, due to shortage of space, the rooms had been full of cases containing exhibits and could not be set out with Brontë furniture as they are today. All this was costly, quite beyond the Society's means without help, but, as in the past, members and the public subscribed handsomely to the appeal for funds, augmented by a generous gift from the Pilgrim Trust. The extension built by Mr. Wade is now used as a library on the ground floor, and an exhibition room.

By 1961 the work was not only completed but paid for, and it is hoped that it will serve the needs of the Society and visitors for many years to come. The Council continues to try and improve facilities and, as time goes on, it is hoped material may be added to the treasure house, and that more relics may return to their rightful home—the Brontë Parsonage Museum.

Plate 9 shows the architect's sketch for the custodian's flat joined to the rear of the Parsonage by a covered way—minor alterations to the flat have since been carried out.

Names of Rooms

Visitors well versed in the books on the Brontës are understandably confused by the names given to the rooms in the house, particularly that of the parlour. To simplify matters for the reader, in this book (plate 13) the room on the *left* as you enter the front door will be referred to as the Dining Room and the room on the right as Mr. Brontë's Study. Confusion has arisen because of the differing accounts given by Mr. Clement Shorter and Mrs. Gaskell. Mr. Shorter's version is based on information given him by Ellen Nussey when an old lady. He writes that on entering the Parsonage "the door on the right leads to Mr. Brontë's study always *called the parlour,* that on the left into the dining room" (14).

Mrs. Gaskell's account is different. She writes "When the Brontës took possession they made the larger *parlour* to the *left* of the entrance the family sitting room (Mr. Shorter says the parlour was the room on the right) while that on the *right* was appropriated by Mr. Brontë as a study. Behind this was the kitchen, behind the former (the dining room) a sort of flagged store room". We must, therefore, treat with caution any reference in books on the Brontës to "the parlour", which may refer to the study or the dining room.

The room behind the dining room was originally a store room and later became Mr. Nicholls' study. It has often been called the peat room but should not be confused with the *peat house* which was in the yard at the back. Mrs. Gaskell refers to this so-called peat room as "a flagged store room".

(14) S.H.B. Vol. 1, p.56, C.S. vol. 1 p.66

Until further information comes to light, it seems advisable to name the rooms as they have been known for many years. The back room on the left as you reach the top of the stairs (over the kitchen) is called Branwell's room and the one on the right (over the store-room—later Mr. Nicholls' study) is called Tabitha's room. Mr. Shorter's account goes on "the room on the *right* as you mount the stairs was allotted to Branwell as a studio". Other accounts have allotted the room on the other side of the landing to Branwell without giving any basis for it. Certainly, as a practical use for a room not accessible to the house from inside, it might well have been handed over to the boy of the family as his painting studio. The evidence is inconclusive.

When the Brontës came to Haworth they were a household of ten and there would be little room to spare. The servants probably slept over the back kitchen. Later, when death had reduced the household, the servants could sleep in the main part of the house. No doubt, as in every household, the family moved to different rooms as circumstances changed.,

Mr. Nicholls' Study and Tabitha's Room.

The small room behind the dining room which Charlotte altered from a store room to a study for her husband was originally only entered from the outside, and the stone framework of the doorway is still visible (plate 15). It had no fireplace until Charlotte built an external chimney.

It was a common practice in the 18th century to have ground floor accommodation for storage and a room above, both only accessible from the outside. This upstairs room would provide sleeping quarters for a man servant (the hind) often employed in the days when travel was by horse, and heavy work, such as pumping and carrying water, had to be done. The room above the store room became Tabitha's bedroom, but originally, again, there was no access to it from the house. This upstairs room would be entered by an outside stone staircase from the yard and the lintel of the outside door to this room is still to be seen on the outside wall (plate 15). At one point below this doorway, near the chimney, can be seen a stone which could be a vestige of the outside stone staircase, marked on the earliest plan (plate 6) as the square on the south-west corner.

It is possible that this part of the Parsonage originally contained

three floors, as the ground level was, at one time, about 1½ft. lower
(15) and there would be no need for rooms of great height. The
room at ground level would be for storage, the room above for a
manservant and above that a hay loft. In Tabitha's room, the old
window and small doorway (only 64" high) to the outside staircase
was uncovered for repairs in 1976. The side of the doorway has now
been covered by glass so that it may be seen by visitors. The base of
this old doorway is 17 inches higher than the existing floor of Tabitha's room. This confirms the opinion that there were originally
three floors in this part of the house instead of the present two.

The ceiling of Mr. Nicholls' study is supported by an old beam,
rough hewn (now boarded over). It would not have been difficult to
raise this at some time, making two storeys instead of three. By doing
this, access to Tabitha's room could then be gained from the landing.
The wall between Tabitha's room and Charlotte's bedroom stops
short at ceiling height, unlike those in the rest of the house, and it is
certain there has been some alteration to this part. The fact that
there was originally only access to the upper room by an outside
staircase is borne out by the dangerous step arrangement at the top
of the main staircase where the door to Tabitha's room was later
inserted. This step is made of wood cleverly camouflaged to look
like stone. A fireplace in the room of the manservant could have been
provided in the gable end where the window now exists and, indeed,
faint smoke traces are to be seen on the outside. This would account
for the third flue in the chimney stack at this side. There is no doubt
that this room would have been suitable as a studio if bedrooms
were in short supply and, it seems, Branwell had a fireplace in his
studio, for one of his friends describes how they used to roast potatoes when discussing his painting.

(15) See chapter on cellars

The House is Built

The Stonework

The front of the house is built of straight cut dressed ashlar stone now a dark grey colour, close jointed millstone grit from the local quarries. The side walls are constructed of random coursed ashlar. When first cut the stone would be a pleasing buff colour, but traces of iron in it oxidise when exposed to the weather and a colour change takes place. The dark grey colour of many a building in the area does not owe all its hue to a sooty atmosphere. The chimneys are constructed of ashlar bedfaced stone, except the chimney stack on the Wade extension, which is random coursed stone, not faced. Examination of the rear and south walls show that the stones are laid in the overshot method (plate 10), each flat stone being laid sloping down towards the outside, so shedding away from the joints any rain water running down the wall. These stones are no tlaid horizontally as those on the front of the house. There are large chamfered quoins at the corners, showing alternately long and short. The window, door casings, front steps and any ornamental features are cut from a fine local stone known as Elland flag.

Great attention has been paid to the stone work, and it reflects the high quality of craftsmanship which has always obtained in the district. A glance at the simple rounded moulding which runs underneath the window sills shows the care that was taken to give a pleasing finish, even though it would hardly be noticed. This moulding is also found—matching the window mould perfectly—underneath the edge of the front doorsteps, and also on the main stairs of the house. It is a charming touch and worthy of study.

The small but handsome and carefully tooled pedimented portico of the front door enhances the front elevation (plate 1). On examination it would appear that it was bought from a local quarry already cut and finished, as the stone work of the surrounding wall shows signs of having been trimmed to receive it. The design of the portico is classical (Renaissance) in style, and was already out of fashion when the house was built. It may perhaps

37

38   Plate 10.   Photograph of side of house showing over-shot walling.

have been lying finished in a stone-mason's yard for some years before it reached the front door of the Parsonage. On the other hand, the student of architecture may, at first glance, accept a date of the early 1770's for the portico and then have difficulty in avoiding the conclusion, on stylistic grounds (such as window sill and stair mouldings), that the house itself was built about 1800. The present author must confess to some difficulty in reconciling stylisticly the architecture of the house with a 1778 date.

The Roof and Charlotte's Alterations

The Parsonage roof is covered with stone flags like many old houses in the district, and was never slated with blue slates. It has a pitch of about 30 degrees, and the gables have heavy stone copings which end horizontally at the foot.

Gutters run along the front and rear of the house supported on stone corbels, all of which appear similar from below but, in fact, are of two different kinds (plate 11). Along the *front* of the house run a series of stone blocks each $3\frac{1}{2}$ft. long which have been cut away at the face forming four corbels, each 3 inches wide and $3\frac{1}{2}$ inches deep, projecting $2\frac{1}{2}$ inches and shaped. At the rear a simpler, cheaper method of supporting the gutter was employed. The corbels are single, individually cut stones of the same outline as the front corbels, set 12 inches directly into the wall and projecting 7 inches on the outside. A good view of these can be obtained from the window on the south wall in the exhibition room above the new Bonnell room.

Examination of the original stone mullioned window on the inside wall shows what was done in the Wade conversion. This window was blocked up and plastered over when covered by the extension at the rear. In order to plaster the wall three corbels were cut off flush with the wall; the cut off ends can clearly be seen near this window, and the old line of the roof gutter can also be traced through. During the alterations of 1958 the plaster was removed and this window was revealed. The former outside portion of this wall shows signs of having been tooled in order to key the plaster of the new room built on to it; this also applies to the wall, the quoins, and the window casing. The stone wall above the window is modern.

There are two main chimney stacks with three flues in each, on

Plate 11. Photographs of corbels carrying the gutters.

the original part of the house. These stacks are of ashlar stonework finished off at the top with a moulding. Mr. Brontë seems to have had a great deal of trouble with his chimneys as they are constantly mentioned by him and the sale catalogue of 1861 has an entry "item 10 chimney top 1/10d". The north chimney stack was rebuilt of coursed rubble wall stone, not being faced like the original stacks, and three more chimneys were added to this north stack to accommodate the rooms in the Wade extension. The stacks were modernised at some time, and fitted with undecorative chimney pots which were removed in 1976. Fortunately, coal or peat fires are no longer needed so no smoke problem arises.

In 1976 the roof was showing signs of age, gales had dislodged some of the flags, and a close inspection revealed a horrible sight. The main roof timbers supporting this heavy roof were in a sad state—they appear in the foreground on plate 15. Sapwood had been used and instead of hardening through the years, the timbers were crumbling away. The main beams were rotten, the purlins too thin and too far apart (23 inches) and the ceiling laths had become friable. The whole roof had to be removed, new beams put in and purlins of double thickness were fitted 16 inches apart. The roof was then felted and boarded in accordance with modern building practice before the stone flags were relaid. Fortunately, the summer of 1976 was exceptionally dry and apart from a thunderstorm, the weather never held up the work. This misfortune (the work was very costly) had its bright side; for the first time since 1850 it was possible to examine the wall structure from above. Long-held suspicions were reinforced by the sight of the old roof timbers. Some, instead of lying firmly across the walls as they originally had done, were resting on a later wall further away, thereby spanning a length greater than that for which they were originally intended. The wall that had been moved back was the wall between Charlotte's bedroom and the nursery.

Descending to the entrance hall, and looking towards the front door, one can see what has been done (plate 12). The strange manner in which the front door is crowded up against the dining room wall indicates that this wall has also been moved, and it has even had to be cut away to allow the door to open to its full extent. The front door, an immoveable fixture, was originally in the middle of the hall outer wall, but is now only 6 inches from the wall of the dining room, while on the other side, 2 feet away from the wall of

Plate 12. Entrance Hall looking towards the front door.

the study. The width of the hall was reduced by 1ft. 6 inches when Charlotte moved the dining room wall further in to the hall (plate 13, the original walling is shown as a dotted line). The wall between the hall and dining room has also been reduced in thickness, making a total gain to the dining room of 3 feet. Note the slight curve in the hall by the front door to allow it to open to its full width. Similar treatment was given to the bedroom wall above (Charlotte's bedroom) and this reduced the size of the children's nursery, or study, by 1 foot 6 inches. The room as it is today would have been much too small for a bed across the window long enough to contain the tall Emily (her coffin measured 5ft. 7inches). Emily's drawing in the nursery shows the bed across the window, a chest on the left wall, and a chair on the right. None of this would be possible in a room the size of the one we see today. The doorway to Charlotte's bedroom originally faced that of the room opposite, and was probably moved at the same time. The house may have had no nursery in its original plan, and the whole area could have been open landing, but by putting a wall and a door across this end of the landing an extra room would be created.

42

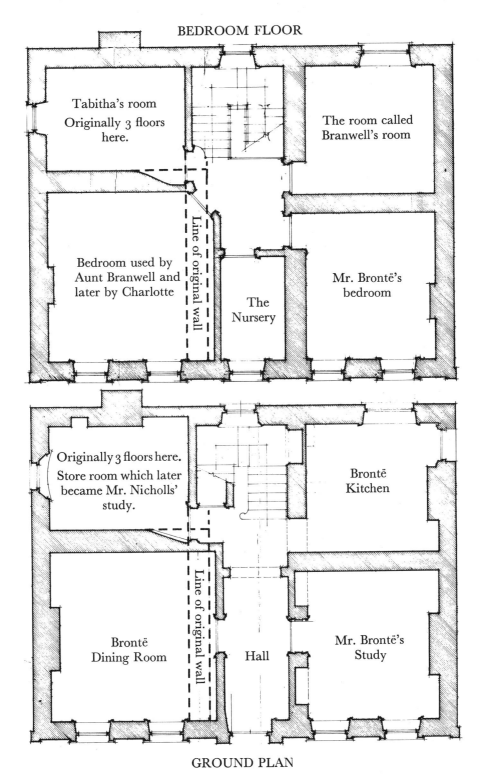

BEDROOM FLOOR

Tabitha's room
Originally 3 floors
here.

The room called
Branwell's room

Bedroom used by
Aunt Branwell and
later by Charlotte

Line of original wall

The
Nursery

Mr. Brontë's
bedroom

Originally 3 floors here.
Store room which later
became Mr. Nicholls'
study.

Brontë
Kitchen

Brontë
Dining Room

Line of original wall

Hall

Mr. Brontë's
Study

GROUND PLAN

Plate 13. Plan of Charlotte's internal alterations.

43

Moving the dining room wall into the hall reduced the width of the hall. Formerly, a chest of drawers stood in the hall, but there is hardly room for one now. The much photographed archway just visible on plate 16 is, however, *equidistant* from the wall of the dining room and that of the study and cannot, therefore, be original. The dining room/hall wall is now much thinner and the original door casing, which would match the charming panelling and soffit in the study door casing, has had to be dispensed with. The different door casings shown in Plate 11 confirm this.

In Mr. Brontë's study there are two round-headed alcoves in the thick wall dividing the study from the hall. These are not of the same height though they were obviously intended to be symmetrical. The archway nearest the window is 3 inches taller than the one on the other side of the door, and it would be interesting to know why this was done. The insertion of the two alcoves does give extra space to the study, but perhaps not as much as Charlotte would have wished. The work could have been done in 1851 for Charlotte, writing to her father from the Smith's home in London on June 7th, says "I fear you will not have had a very comfortable week in the dining room, but by this time I suppose the parlour [Mr. Brontë's study] reformation will be nearly completed, and you will soon be able to return to your old quarters" (16). As usual, poor Mr. Brontë had to deal with the workmen in Charlotte's absence.

Work of this magnitude could have been done at any time, but the task would be more easily carried out whilst the weight of the roof was removed in 1850 and there is, therefore, a strong presumption that the walls were moved at this time. As the detective would say "Here was the opportunity—what was the motive?".

By 1850 Charlotte was no longer just the parson's daughter, but a famous and prosperous authoress. In her youth she had been a governess in fine houses and, in her success, she was invited to the homes of the rich and famous and she would be expected to return some of this hospitality. With money in her purse why should she not improve the Parsonage? She had already ordered William Wood to provide new furniture throughout the house and a larger "withdrawing room" would be splendid for entertaining. Henceforth the dining room would become Charlotte's sitting room.

In May 1850, Charlotte set off on her travels, not returning until the dust had settled in mid July. She went to London, Birstall, and Edinburgh and then back to Birstall. Apparently poor Mr. Brontë, who in later life expressed his distaste for having work done in the house, was left with Martha and other helpers to deal with this alone. The house was now being re-roofed. Charlotte writes "I cannot come home for the house is now unroofed". The operation was of such a magnitude that William Wood was called in to remove much of the furniture and his account reads, "To P. Bronty. To furneter removing ½ day 1/9d June 15th 1850" and significantly adds "To 1 set of stand steps 5/9d". Charlotte wrote to her father on June 4th 1850 from the home of the Smiths in London where she was staying "I was glad to get your letter this morning, and still more glad to learn that your health continues in some degree to improve. I fear you will feel the present weather somewhat debilitating, at least if it is as warm in Yorkshire as in London. I cannot help grudging these fine days on account of the roofing of the house. It is a great pity the workmen were not prepared to begin a week ago" (17).

On June 12th she writes to Martha Brown that the house will be now in a bustle of unroofing warning her and Martha Redman, not to lift heavy weights, or go out without caps, or otherwise "take measures to make yourselves ill. I was rather curious to, know how you managed about a sleeping place for yourself and Tabby". By July 15th she returned home to find, to her annoyance Martha, Tabby and her father in a "sad pitch of nervous excitement and alarm" but dismissed this as having small cause (18). Mr. Brontë took a different view, for he writes to Ellen Nussey that he is in better health "and that after a host of labour amidst decayed laths and rafters and broken lime plaster and busy carpenters, *masons* and repairers of various descriptions, we have at length got our house put in order . . . tell Charlotte that with due affection I hope soon to see her". The tidying up process was still going on in August.

Whether the doorway to Tabitha's room was broken through at this time is not known, but in 1854 Charlotte was again busy turning the storeroom into a study for her husband-to-be, Mr. Nicholls. She saw clearly that he and her father would get on more agreeably if each had his own domain. On May 22nd she wrote that "the green and white curtains are up; they exactly suit the paper". In order to make Mr. Nicholls comfortable in his study, a fire-place was built with an outside chimney which necessitated blocking half the stone mullioned window in his room also the one above in Tabitha's

(17) S.H.B. 564, C.S. 444
(18) S.H.B. 572, C.S. 449

room and in order to give light to these a window was put in each room in the gable end.

Thunder and Lightning

On December 12th 1824 the Rev. P. Brontë preached a sermon "in reference to an EARTHQUAKE and extraordinary Eruption of Mud and Water" that had taken place ten days before "on the moors of that Chapelry" (19). He went on to describe how he sent out the children in the evening for a walk with the servant, when the heavens began "to blacken fast". Watching from the window he heard a distant explosion of thunder, and "a gentle tremor in the chamber in which he was standing and in the glass of the window before him". He goes on to say that these manifestations are the Lord's method of chastising man. He describes the lamentations for the great expense to which the inhabitants would be put adjuring

(19) Histories of the area record a violent storm in September 1824 which did widespread damage.

Plate 14. Photograph of Parsonage taken after 1859, showing window glazing bars and clay chimney.

them that Providence had sent it "to arouse the graceless persons of Haworth and district to a contemplative frame of mind and no longer to indulge in their bad passions and practices". This phenomenon was watched by Mr. Brontë from a window in the Parsonage commanding a view towards Ponden.

Mr. Brontë had installed a lightning conductor on the south chimney of the house (plate 1) and during the roof repairs in 1976, examination showed that the lightning conductor had perished and it was removed for repair. Three days later, on a brilliant June afternoon, three men working on the roof observed the "heavens to blacken fast". In a great hurry they struggled to cover temporarily the existing roof cavity with plastic sheeting. Suddenly there was an "explosion"—lightning had struck—the three on the roof were stunned and though unharmed, were much shaken. No damage was done to the Parsonage but thousands of pounds worth of damage was done to the Baptist Chapel a hundred yards away. The member of the Council, to whom we are indebted for plate 6, and who had done a deal of hard work on behalf of the Society throughout the operation, was one of the unfortunates. Surely Mr. Brontë would have adjured us all "to be grateful we are spared". Perhaps the message is—never tamper with Mr. Brontë's lightning conductor—he might have considered it one of the bad practices against which he gave such awful warning.

Cellars

The cellars under the house extend beneath the kitchen and the present Library. The only original eighteenth century cellar is the room beneath the kitchen. The present Library is the large room in the north wing added by Mr. Wade and labelled on the plan (plate 7) as the "New Dining Room". He must have required greater cellar accommodation than that provided under the old kitchen (called Hall on plate 7) and so added a large cellar beneath the Library. This cellar is entered from the smaller one under the old kitchen through a doorway which was originally a window to an outside area. The remains of the stone window casing are clearly visible today. The window bottom in the old cellar would be near ground level, the cellar floor being about four feet below. This was the cellar in which Aunt Branwell brewed the beer which she insisted on fetching herself to the pique of the servants. Access to the cellar was originally through a door in the hall beneath the half landing of the staircase. Under the main staircase of the house was an open area having a door on the right to the cellar and another straight ahead to the back yard which was later altered into a window. The original level of the back yard can be seen at the turn of the cellar stairs.

Windows and Window Tax.

The windows at the front of the house are sash windows of traditional proportions of the late 18th and early 19th centuries, and fitted with shutters on the inside. The sills, jambs and lintels standing proud of the wall surface, are of fine smooth ashlar with a simple running mould under the sill.

The windows at the rear of the house were of a different design. Instead of sashes they were mullioned casements, a pattern much used in the district throughout the 17th and 18th centuries in farmhouses and cottages. These were 5ft. wide by 4ft. high, divided into two lights by a stone mullion of V-shaped section. Each light would originally be divided into small panes fixed in metal or wood. The rear windows were blocked up by alterations made by the Brontës, but at what date is not known. The outline of the window in the store room is still partially discernible on the outside of the wall near the chimney built after Charlotte transformed this room into a study for Mr. Nicholls (plate 15).

The window in Tabitha's room has a rounded arch on the inside. The stonework on the outside of these two windows is not identical, indicating that they were inserted at different times.

Mr. Brontë made alterations to the rear of the Parsonage, but exactly when or what he did is not known. There are one or two indications, but they are by no means conclusive. For example, Mr. Brontë records that his house tax in 1851 was £10–13–0d. "formerly I paid only £7–0–0d. or nearly". So his rateable value may have been increased, or the rates may have been raised. In 1843 the rateable value of the house was £6–6–10d and at 1/8d. in the £ the rates Mr. Brontë paid amounted to 10/6d.

There was a general up-grading of rateable value between 1850 and 1852 as the returns prove. In May 1850 Mr. Brontë's rates were 1/8d. in the £ when his house was valued at £7–13–5d. and the amount he had to pay was 12/9d. Two years later the rates had come down to 1/-d. in the £, but his property had been revalued at £10–13–0d. so he paid 10/8d. John Brown's house across the lane was valued in 1850 at £2–10–7d. and in 1852 the valuation had increased to £4–16–0d. This, taken in conjunction with other properties in the area, makes it clear that it is incorrect to assume that, because the rateable value had been raised, alterations to the Parsonage had taken place (20).

In 1831 Mr. Brontë paid tax on 13 windows, and in 1845 he paid for "three windows more". Window tax was first levied in 1697 and was not repealed until 1851 when a rate on the value of the property was levied. The law stipulated that a window was taxable unless it had either been blocked up by the same material as the surrounding wall, or unless the part blocked was divided by metal or stone from the unblocked part. (One could not avoid tax by dividing up and blocking part of a wooden framed window). Blocking up one of the two sections in the mullioned window in Tabitha's room saved Mr. Brontë tax on one window because the

(20) Information by courtesy of Keighley Rate Office

Plate 15. Part view of rear of Parsonage.

two lights were divided by a stone mullion.. Each section of window divided by a stone mullion was chargeable. Tax avoidance explains why many old windows of this type can be found with a stone mullion cut out or a section filled in. It follows that counting up windows is a dubious way of assessing Mr. Brontë's building activities. All we know for certain is that in 1831 he paid tax on 13 windows, and in 1845 he paid tax on 16 windows, but how this figure was arrived at is not known. It is possible that at this time he made alterations to the house, but no records are yet available.

Changes in the law on window tax in 1851 encouraged many people to open up old windows and insert new ones. The invention of the method of making sheet glass by rolling substantially reduced the cost of glass and was a further inducement. Large panes of glass had previously been costly and this explains why, for economy, the rear windows of the Parsonage were much smaller than those at the front.

Repairs in Tabitha's room in 1976 involved removing the plasterwork covering the old mullioned window. Behind the plaster was found the original stone mullioned window, corresponding to the window of the same type in Branwell's room. At the side of the window in Tabitha's room, a doorway was found which gave access to the stone staircase on the outside. An inspection of the rear wall of the Parsonage also confirms this. On the south-west corner can be seen evidence of this outside doorway and window (plate 15).

It would be safe to assume that a window of the same type lit the kitchen beneath Branwell's room, and that a similar window lit the storeroom below Tabitha's room. The small rooflight in Branwell's room was put in to light this room when Mr. Wade made it into a passageway. The pointed Gothic archway gave access to Mr. Wade's new domestic quarters and did not exist in the time of the Brontës.

Anyone interested in examining the stone lintel still embedded in the rear wall outside on the first floor near Branwell's room will notice that this lintel is machine cut, and is likely, therefore, to have been put in by Mr. Wade, whereas the windows existing in the time of the Brontës are of hand cut stone.

The house as originally built contained nine windows at the front as they stand today. At the rear there was a long window with round arched top on the staircase, set between two pairs of mullioned windows each of two lights but, as already mentioned, only one in Branwell's room remains revealed.

The staircase window was originally much longer, the base being raised some time between 1872 and 1936. The original stone sill is still in place, and a part of it can be seen from the outside 3ft. lower than the present window bottom. This window, known as the Oxford pattern, was not in general use before 1830 and is therefore, unlikely to be original. The photograph on plate 15 shows the original outline. The staircase window originally extended below the half landing which may in the first place have been constructed leaving a space between the half landing and the window which was protected by a handrail and bannisters across it

Wainscot and Staircase

When examining a house built in 1778 in this part of the country one expects to find certain features. One of these is a wood wainscot or panelling running round the walls to a height of between 2ft. 6 inches to 3ft., but fashion and changes in building techniques caused the wainscot to diminish in height and eventually to become the skirting board. Often a wooden mould was put on the wall at waist height as a vestige of the old practice of wainscotting. Mr. Charles Hale on his visit in 1861 says that he carried away "plenty of the mouldings or woodwork that went round the rooms". Running a hand along the plasterwork of the rooms one felt, in places, an uneven surface, indicating that a wainscot has been removed and plastered over at a later date. Many cottages in the area still contain the boarded wainscot, as no doubt it was a practical way of keeping out draughts and was more durable than plaster. The waist-rail in the hall was put there in 1958 to restore its original appearance as far as possible.

Alterations to the floor level carried out by Mr. Wade would involve the removal of the wainscot which was replaced by a narrow skirting board and "a quantity of rotten wood was thrown out". Mrs. Gaskell says that "the Parsonage was built at a time when wood was plentiful, as the massive stair bannisters, *the wainscots,* and the heavy frames testify". Clement Shorter writes "The staircase with its solid bannister remains as it did half a century ago". It seems an extraordinary description of the staircase as we now see it, for the bannister and handrail are unusually light and

51

slender and curiously, some of the bannister rails are metal and some are wood. Certainly the staircase window bottom has been raised and this may have been done when the cellar head was walled in (plate 16), but it is also possible that the whole staircase was at some time renewed.

The staircase, with other features of the house, seems to be of a design that architecturally suggests a period much later than 1778 and invites the question—is it original? Standing on the staircase and looking around one can ask, is there anything to be seen which suggests that this is how it was built in 1778? The staircase, the archway, the bannisters, are more in the style of the first half of the 19th century than the last quarter of the 18th.

There would be no picture rails in the house when it was built since they did not come into general use until after the mid-nineteenth century.

Plasterwork

The many changes that have taken place since the Parsonage was built in 1778 have resulted in the destruction of some early features, one of these casualties being the plasterwork. Apart from the kitchen, it is clear that the ceilings and cornices have, at various times, been completely renewed. The kitchen ceiling, however, appears of original design, the thick moulded cornice being typical of the period and is found nowhere else in the original part of the house.

The moulded cornice in the kitchen is 'returned' just inside the hall/kitchen doorway, indicating that originally there was a doorway leading from the kitchen to Mr. Brontë's study. The pointed arch leading from kitchen to hall is an adaptation of the original doorway which was made by Mr. Wade.

The bedroom ceilings and cornices were renewed in 1976 and those found there have been faithfully reproduced.

As has already been said, the archway in the hall just visible in plate 16 could not be original to the house, as the wall of the dining room was much further back. The pointed arch on the staircase containing the clock was put in by Mr. Wade to provide access to his new bathroom. The same applies to the archways in Branwell's room.

Plate 16.   View of staircase and cellar door.

Decoration and Furnishing

The alterations in 1958 made it possible to replace the family furniture in the rooms from which it had been removed nearly 100 years before. The show cases were moved into the new extension and the dining room and Mr. Brontë's study were restored as far as possible to their appearance in the time of the Brontës. The catalogues of the furniture sold in 1861, and at subsequent sales, have been of value in establishing the authenticity of the items on display. Other rooms contain items not formerly used in the Parsonage but having Brontë connections. For example, the late 17th century Spanish sacristy cupboard, known as the "Apostles" cupboard, was seen by Charlotte and is described in detail in "Jane Eyre". The clock on the half landing is not the one Mr. Brontë used to wind on his way to bed (and which, together with his watch, he had cleaned at a charge of 2/6d), but one of a similar type made by a local clockmaker.

Research into the decoration of the house has been made possible by the removal of old plasterwork during alterations in recent years. In 1976 repairs to the wall in Tabitha's room revealed the window blocked up by the Brontës when the chimney was built on the outside wall. At the side of this window the old plaster was found to have been painted in an amateur fashion in matt paint. The colours used were a sea green flecked with rose pink, and it is interesting to speculate whether this was some of Branwell's handiwork when, according to Ellen Nussey, he used this room as a studio.

The room across the landing over the kitchen on the left as you ascend the second flight of stairs contains the window blocked up by Mr. Brontë. A large cupboard had been secured to the wall covering the blocked up window, and in this cupboard was a box containing dresses which had belonged to the sisters. Behind this cupboard on the wall and window reveal was found wallpaper which is reproduced on the cover of this book. The paper has a white ground with grey foliate scrolls in a trellis pattern ornamented with tiny flowers in bright blue and pink. This paper, and the patterns found in Charlotte's writing desk (plate 22) have been a valuable guide to the kind of wallpaper the Brontës used in the Parsonage. In May 1843 William Wood charged Mr. Brontë 5/–d for papering and sizing a room (21).

The painting of the outside of the house may have been Mr. Brontë's responsibility, though this would have been unusual. His notebook has a receipt from John Hudson, July 1852, for £1 which must have been good value, for, although it was 2/–d more than Mr. Brontë paid in 1848, it included painting "all his windows, gates, doors, water spouts and water tubs, to suffice for two years".

Mrs. Gaskell, who only visited the Parsonage once during Charlotte's lifetime, writes that the dining room, when she visited, was decorated in crimson. Certainly Charlotte put up crimson curtains for in December 1851 she wrote "We have got curtains for the dining room. I ordered them at the factory to be dyed crimson, but they are badly dyed and do not please me". A Diary Paper describes Emily as lying reading on the hearth rug before the dining room fire and giving a succinct statement of her philosophy. The famous "Gun Group" (plate 17) shows the family sitting at a

(21) See William Wood's accounts. Appendix 1

Plate 17.   The 'Gun Group' by Branwell Bronte.

table with a background of a patterned wallpaper with vertical stripes. This, according to legend, was painted about 1837 but unfortunately the picture had disappeared by 1894.

Ellen Nussey, in 1871, recounted that when she first visited Charlotte in 1833 the walls were painted "a pretty dove coloured tint" and not papered. This description would correspond with a discovery of the colour of the woodwork (which would include the wainscot) made in 1958 when the alterations were in progress. The decorators were asked to strip the layers of paint from the doors in the hall with great care. These doors are of the usual six panelled type used in the Georgian period, but the quality of the woodwork in the Parsonage falls a long way behind that of the stonework. The doors were of thin timber and cheap construction. In a house of higher quality the doors would have a raised bead within the fielded panels. A substitute for this was to paint a line so as to emphasise the proportions of the panel. In 1958, after layers of paint had been carefully removed, a ground work of pale bluish grey best described as "starch blue" was revealed and as expected, each panel had painted on it a black line with a square at each corner (plate 18). Faint traces of this lining are still discernible in places.

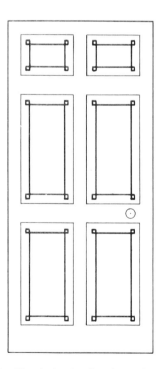

Plate 18.   Sketch showing line decoration of doors.

Mr. Brontë's notebook records that "In 1850 and 1851 I got the rooms painted and stained for just about £4 and from what I have seen they ought to do for at least 1860". Care should be taken in interpreting these words as "staining" is a term used by painters for the colour they mix in paint. It has been assumed that this was the brown grained colour used in Edwardian times to simulate grained wood, but blue, red, or any other colours were referred to as stains. As the rooms were wainscotted and the windows shuttered, there would be a considerable amount of woodwork to be painted. Putting wallpaper above the wainscot was not an expensive item. As we see from his bill, William Wood papered and sized a room for 5/-d so it is unwise to assume that all the rooms had painted walls, as this is not borne out by the evidence. Wallpaper was a way of covering plasterwork with an inexpensive and ornamental covering. "In Mr. Brontë's time anyone who cared to visit was welcome to see the little room with its ugly wallpaper, simple furniture, and the scanty collection of books". (22)

On May 22nd 1854 Charlotte had completed transforming the store room into a study for her husband-to-be and wrote to Ellen Nussey "the little new room is got into order and the green and white curtains are up; they exactly suit the paper and look clean and neat enough".

Ellen Nussey states "There was not much carpet anywhere except in the sitting room and on the study floor.." Charlotte in her "History of the Year" 1829 says "Emily is in the parlour brushing the carpet" and at the sale of house effects when Mr. Brontë died, a quantity of rugs and carpets was sold, including a stair carpet, as the short extract from the catalogue shows (23). Ellen Nussey also recalled that there "was no drapery of any kind" but the sale catalogue records the sale of window blinds, bed hangings, cornice and curtains. Furthermore, Charlotte's two pictures of Flossy sitting on the Parsonage window seat show a thin blue curtain draped at the window (plate 20). Ellen Nussey first visited Haworth in 1833 and she came many times to visit her old school friend. Her recollections of the Parsonage as she first saw it were printed long after in "*Scribner's Monthly*", an American magazine, in 1871.

The Society has collected together many pieces of furniture formerly belonging to the Brontës, including the piano supplied by John Green of London in 1834. It was later sold at Sotheby's in December 1916 and is of interest to the connoisseurs of old musical

(22) Horsfall Turner "Haworth Past and Present" p.156
(23) See Appendix 2

instruments because of its design. Branwell had a violin which later became the property of John Robinson of Wombwell and would be a welcome addition to the Museum if it could be found (24).

When Charlotte was in London in 1851 she wrote to her father "I am glad the parlour is done . . . but am quite shocked to hear of the piano being dragged up into the bedroom—there it must necessarily be absurd and in the parlour it looked so well, besides being convenient for your books. I wonder why you don't like it?". She would be glad to know that Emily's piano is now back in its rightful place.

The drawing of a scene in the Parsonage in Emily's Diary Paper of 1837 shows the sisters seated at a large table with a writing box and papers. The table with its straight legs could be of an earlier design than the one now standing in the dining room, though the chairs in the picture could well be those now on show. There are two tables placed together and covered with a cloth in Mr. Brontë's study and a large table in the dining room. These three tables were made to fit together and form one large dining table and could well have been made by William Wood.

Mrs. Gaskell records that Charlotte's sense of order was such "that she could not carry on a conversation if a chair were out of place". The set of six handsome chairs in Mr. Brontë's study date from the last quarter of the 18th century, so would have been considered out of fashion when Charlotte refurnished. She must have rightly felt that chairs of this quality were too good to discard; these are likely to be the chairs sold when Mr. Nicholls left, at 17/-d each.

Charles Hale writes that Charlotte gave an order to William Wood "to renew the furniture of the house from top to bottom throughout with his own make" (25). Certainly the dining table, chairs and sofa are of the kind that would be made by a Haworth cabinet maker of the 1850's. The horse-hair sofa in the dining room was sold in 1861 for £3/12/od and the dining table and chairs made £5.

Mrs. Gaskell recalls book shelves standing between the windows in Mr. Brontë's study and Charlotte, writing to her father, mentions books being placed on top of the piano. The 1861 sale catalogue contains a large quantity of books, which must have required more accommodation, certainly than the bookcase which was sold for 2/6d. The walls were hung with pictures which, according to the sale catalogue, must have been prints of the Martin paintings of Old

(24) Leeds Mercury 7.X.1906
(25) B.S.T. vol. 15 p.131

Testament phenomena—"Deluge" "Joshua and the Sun" "Passage over the Red Sea" "Belshazzar's Feast"—all are so recorded together with "Large Oil Paintings and other pictures".

Unfortunately, the Society has been able to recover little of the bedroom furniture. There was a small camp bed which cannot be traced but may well be the one sold at the sale and drawn by Emily in the sketch on her Diary Paper of 1845 which can be seen at the Museum in the (now much smaller) room over the hall. Branwell is recorded as having set his bed curtains on fire, which indicates he slept either in a four poster or half-tester bed. The sale at Sotheby's in 1916 of Brontë relics records "2 long fluted oak bed posts from Charlotte Brontë's bedstead with the head and hangings for the bed". Other pieces of furniture in the Museum were sold by Wooller Jennings in January 1888 at Saltaire, which were formerly the property of Mr. Benjamin Binns; these were authenticated as having come from the original sale at Haworth Parsonage.

More information on the furnishings can be gleaned from Appendix 1 listing the accounts of William Wood which are printed exactly as written. The number of times William was called on to repair chairs, doors, locks etc., sheds a curious light on life at the Parsonage and seem to be particularly frequent during Branwell's later life. Some of the terms used and the phonetic spelling may puzzle those not used to the North country dialect. For this reason the outer column is added to clarify the subject.

Family Finance

Charlotte wrote to Robert Southey in 1837 "My father is a clergy-man of limited though competent means". This is a fair assessment of the position and the impression that the Brontës were poor is not borne out by the facts, as shown by details of Mr. Brontë's tax account for 1831 given by Mr. George Crowther (26). The total tax collected in Haworth in 1831 was £117-19-3d; of this the school master paid 8/-d, Mr. Brontë paid £4-19-9d, of which £1-3-6d, was for hair powder and 8/-d was tax for keeping a house dog. Window tax accounted for the largest proportion £2-13-3d, being tax on 13 windows. In his notebook he made an entry "I formerly paid £2-6-7d. half yearly. In 1845 I had to pay for three windows more, all of which I have, and for hair powder and dogs (by way of surcharge to Mr. Wm. Garnett). The next half year will be only £2-15-5½d. Paid to Mr. Ogden April 1848 £3-11-6d. 1845 rateable value of my house £7-13-5d. gross estimate £9-4-1d. Assessed taxes paid to Mr. Whalley £11-6-0d. on May 5th 1851". The rate per £ was assessed each year.

Mr. Brontë's letter to the Governors of Queen Anne's Bounty shows he had an income of "about £180 a year besides the surplice fees of about £14 a year". He was, however, well aware that the income of £180 was payable by the Trustees and that he was de-pendent on them for this amount. The arrangement for paying an incumbent was unusual. Mr. Brontë rightly asserts that his only income from the church was his surplice fees, for the rest he must look to the Trustees some of whom were Dissenters. Any curate employed would initially be at his own expense, but a grant for this was paid by the Church Pastoral Aid Society. Mr. Brontë records in his notebook that he received a grant of £80 a year to pay his curate, but, judging this inadequate, pressed for it to be raised to £100 and was successful in his application.

The Terrier of 1781 (plate 2) records that the Minister received the rents, issues, profits arising from five farms in the Stanbury district and *full* dues for all kinds of ecclesiastical duties. It seems a compromise about the payment of some of these dues had been reached with the Vicar of Bradford when Mr. Brontë came to Haworth, and on his appointment agreed to take only half of the dues collected for Marriages, Funerals, Baptisms and Churchings, and to pay the other half at Easter to the Vicar of Bradford. His notebook records "For 1851 the whole of the dues, after deductions were made, was £10-5-6d, half of which £5-2-9d. was sent to the Vicar of Bradford".

Mr. Brontë's entries on the Enquiry carried out by the Church Commissioners in August 1832 show that "One curate is occasionally employed" and "the curate's stipend at that time was from £50-£70 a year". "The Gross Amount of the Annual Income of the Benefice . . . on an average of three years past" is given as varying "from £170-£180 a year, but there are usually eight or ten pounds deducted for repairs". There was no other source of income apart from the "Surplice and other Fees" some of which were retained by Mr. Brontë—in 1832 he kept £7. The report states that Mr. Brontë's net income was "just about one hundred and seventy pounds". On August 25th 1828 Mr. Brontë wrote to Richard Burn, the Secretary of Queen Anne's Bounty asking for an augmentation of his stipend. This was refused as his income exceeded the statutory minimum of £150 required to qualify for a grant.

Finally, when asked whether or not this sum is likely to be increased in the coming year (1833) Mr. Brontë adds this comment "I think the annual income will probably be less—*as much repairs are wanted* of a very expensive nature". From this it appears the incumbent was responsible for repairs and dependent on the Trustees for re-imbursement. If this letter refers to the roof Mr. Brontë had to wait a long time, as it was not until 1850 that he was able to have a new roof. A letter from the Rev. John Wade to Robert Heaton, a Patron of the living and a Trustee, says that he "has made good all other dilapidations which Mr. Brontë was answerable for".

Mr. Brontë was a generous man and subscribed as much as he could afford to charity and, as recorded in his Will, sent frequent sums to his relatives back in Ireland. Charlotte supported various charities though "regrets she will have to cut this down for a short time". Emily, when the school project was languishing, did not feel anxious about their finances. She writes "We have cash enough for our present wants with prospects of an accumulation" though Emily's tiny writing in a partially destroyed account book has an entry "I exceed my income by £12-10-0d besides being answerable for

£163-18-10d December 1845" and "January 1846 expenses £20".
What accounts for the large amount for which she is answerable
also the prospect of an accumulation, is not certain, but alterations
to the house were at the time contemplated. The school project was
being considered and the sisters may have earmarked a large sum
for this purpose. The scheme, however, was dropped and no alterations were made; Charlotte says it would be foolish to do anything
as they had no prospect of getting any pupils. Charlotte's financial
adventure in railway stock (this was the time of "railway mania")
was not successful.

Most of the clothing was made at home. Material having been
bought, the girls spent many hours in Aunt Branwell's room stitching
away. Mr. Bronte continued to patronise the tailor he had in his
Cambridge days, occasionally having a suit "turned" by the
Haworth tailor who inserted special inside pockets for his famous
pistols (27). The Parsonage house was rent free to the incumbent
during his lifetime and this was a cause of anxiety to his daughters.
There was always plenty of domestic help available in the house and
the servants were paid a wage in addition to their keep. Their
wages were small; for example, in January 1846 Mr. Brontë raised
Martha Brown's wages from 2/3d per week to 2/6d—in 1855 he
was paying her £9 a year.

In 1829 Branwell took up drawing and an art teacher was employed at great expense. The girls went to the Clergy Daughters'
School at Cowan Bridge at a charge of £14 a year for board and
education, and after a spell at home were then sent to Miss Wooler's
school at Roe Head. The cost of this was met by Charlotte's god-
mother Mrs. Thomas Atkinson, wife of the Vicar of Thornton and
by Charlotte returning to teach in exchange for free schooling for
one of her sisters.

The fatal illness of his wife was a drain on Mr. Brontë's resources,
but this was alleviated by the astonishing generosity of friends and
strangers, who showed in this practical way how highly Mr. Brontë
was esteemed. After her death, he writes to the Vicar of Dewsbury on
November 27th 1821 telling his friend the sad news and saying how
touched he was at the gifts of money he received. He had received
from friends in Bradford over £150, a donation of £50 from a
London Society and a further £50 from a kind friend, added to
which he received another £150 from other friends.

When Mrs. Brontë died Aunt Branwell came from Penzance to

(27) Bradford Observer 17 II 1894

run the house and look after the children. Aunt Branwell had an annuity of £50 a year, and she paid a share of the household expenses for the 21 years she lived at Haworth. Since the first payment of her annuity in 1808 she had received £1,700, a considerable sum in those days. She kindly gave financial help to the children and their father, favours that she liked to "confer in style". On her death she left her money divided in equal shares between the Brontë sisters and her niece in Penzance. She left her Japan dressing box to Branwell, and with that he had to be content. An income from property owned by Aunt Branwell in Penzance was left to the Brontës and on May 8th 1846 Charlotte writes acknowledging receipt of the rents due as their share.

Charlotte was always determined that the family should safeguard against their financial future. Mr. Brontë's income would die with him and the girls feared for the future when they would have to vacate the Parsonage and find a new home. How sad that, after taking so much thought for the morrow, death intervened, and the morrow took care of itself. Their father outlived them all.

Living in the House

Cleanliness

Mr. Brontë always took an interest in public health, and fought long with the authorities to obtain good supplies of piped water for his parishioners. He was well informed on all matters of sanitation and water pollution, and would surely have given the health of his family his first attention. The water supply to his own house was from a well fed from the hillside above. At that time there was no building or graveyard above the source of the well, and, though William Wood had supplied a well cover on November 24th 1845 at a cost of 8d, it seems someone had been careless. A record in Mr. Brontë's notebook reads "Sept. 1847 got the well cleaned by pump sinker and two men for 5/-d. The water tinged yellow by eight tins in a state of decomposition. It had not been cleaned for twenty years or more". Water from the well was pumped by hand to two points. The well was still in existence in the time of Mr. Wade. The *Keighley Herald* reported that "Mr. Hartley Greenwood broke sand and pumped water at the Parsonage". This water was placed in pails in the passage room and boiled in the fireside boiler in the kitchen. These were the pails of water Emily used to put out the flames when Branwell set light to his bed curtains. The water from the roof was collected in troughs from the "heve spout" (the eave spouting) repaired by William Wood who had supplied the "truf and cock" (tap) for 1/4d.

Washing facilities would be provided by cans of hot water in jug and basin in the bedroom. The sale catalogue of the household effects lists "picher and Bowl 1/2d . . . washstands 3/9d. and 5/-d". A washstand, ewer and basin, can still be seen in Tabitha's room.

Ellen Nussey sent Charlotte a shower bath which was supplied by Nelsons of Leeds, William Wood fitting it with "knobs" for 2/6d in 1849. Charlotte wrote to Ellen promising that when she came "she should have a drenching in her own shower".

A privy, or earth closet, is discernible to a keen eye on some old photographs of the Parsonage. As shown on plate 8, it stood against the south wall of the back yard and contained a large seat and a small one for a child. Mr. Wade stated there was no bathroom or water closet when he took over. A night commode appears in the sale catalogue of 1861 and brought the high price of 5/-d. Household linen was washed by Sally Mosley in the back kitchen in wash tubs stirred with a peggy stick (William Wood repaired it for 6d in 1842) and then put through a mangle which appears in the 1861 sale for £1-9-0d. According to Emily the girls shared the ironing and "turning" which meant putting the damp clothes through the mangle. In the days when quantities of cotton and woollen under-clothes were worn there would be a great deal to do. The water had to be pumped and heated by the fire.

Warmth

On December 21st 1839 Charlotte wrote to Ellen Nussey, "I manage the ironing and keep the rooms clean. Emily does the baking and attends to the kitchen". Charlotte invoked Aunt Branwell's wrath by scorching the clothes; it seems much of the ironing was done upstairs, the irons, no doubt, being heated on the fire in Aunt Branwell's (later Charlotte's) bedroom. One of these irons was put to good use when Emily was bitten by a dog, for she cauterized the wound with one of Tabitha's "Italian" irons. Charlotte and Ellen Nussey used to sit before the bedroom fire curling each other's hair with tongs. There was evidently gas in the house when Mr. Wade made alterations in the 1870's as he specified that existing gas pipes and fittings were to be made good. A gas fire was included in the sale in 1861. Mr. Brontë's notebook shows that he paid bills for gas but it is not stated whether they were for the house or church.

Mrs. Gaskell writes with pleasure of the bright fires burning all over the house. The old grates were found lying in the cellar in 1958 and one was put in place of a late 19th century grate in Mr. Brontë's study. The stone fireplace was reconstructed by Mr. Harold Mitchell in 1956, but lacks the iron cheeks, hobs and back plate which customarily covered the stone work round the fire. An Edwardian fireplace in the dining room was replaced by a marble mantelpiece dating from about 1820 from a dressing room in Methley Hall in 1958. A grate of the early 19th century was found and inserted to give an impression of the room as it would have been when Anne used to sit with her feet on the fender (now to be seen in place) to the vexation of her aunt—"Anne, where are your feet?" reply "On the floor".

Mrs Brontë made a pathetic request in her last illness to be lifted up in her bed to see the grate cleaned "in the Cornish way". This grate in her bedroom has a cove of a type not often seen in this part of the country and may have been installed by Mr. Brontë in an effort to combat a smoky chimney. He seems to have fought a running battle with the winds of heaven, as there is frequent reference to chimney cowls of various kinds. In despair he writes he will settle for "blowers as it is cheaper than taking down the whole chimney". This refers to the peculiar tall chimney rising from the kitchen wing on old photographs. This chimney appears to be made entirely of fireclay and must have been a last stand against the fury of the Haworth winds, though it did nothing to add to the appearance of the house. Miss Branwell missed the mild Cornish climate and is reputed to have overheated her room to the detriment of the health of the sisters. When going to the kitchen or the yard she put on wooden pattens over her slippers; she found the passage rooms very cold. One of the pattens is on show in the Museum, and seems a practical way of crossing cold or damp floors whilst still wearing slippers. The poignant account of Emily's death told by Mary F. Robinson says that Emily, determined to the last to feed her dogs "got up walking slowly, holding out in her thin hands an apronful of broken meat and bread. When she reached the flagged passage the cold took her, she staggered on the uneven pavement and fell against the wall".

Food and Drink

In 1861 Mrs. Beeton's Book of Household Management was published with recipes and bills of fare which would today be beyond either the means or scope of the average housewife. Times have changed, but for half a century Mrs. Beeton's rich food was consumed at many an English table groaning with courses of fish and meat. No wonder Clement Shorter could write that the diet of the Brontës was "of the simplest. A *single* joint followed by one kind or another of milk pudding". No mention of the apple pudding of which Emily speaks with pleasant anticipation, or Mrs. Clapham's gift of pigeon (28) that Mr. Brontë so enjoyed. There is plenty of evidence that the Brontë table was well supplied and Mrs. Gaskell's

66

statement that the family lived largely on potatoes is not borne out by the evidence.

The small tithe paid to the parson of dairy produce, meat and eggs etc., disappeared in the Commutation Act of 1836, but the tradition of sending small gifts to the parson lingered on well into the 20th century. Parishioners must have often wished to express gratitude for help in times of distress. Preserves, game, fish, vegetables and dairy produce, must have been sent to the back door of the Parsonage by kindly, grateful neighbours and friends of Mr. Brontë and in the same spirit, work done by the local tradesman would be charged at a low price. This augmentation of the larder was an added benefit to any incumbent when food was the major cost of living.

Ellen Nussey seems frequently to have sent pots of "crab cheese" and there is mention of her excellent potted tongue. "Lord John Manners brought in his hand two brace of grouse for papa" (29). The Ferrands were generous in their gifts of game, Mr. Brontë exclaiming at the great size of some of the birds.

Mr. Brontë himself was a keen shot and taught Emily to shoot at a target in the garden. He wrote to Mr. Ferrand "thank you for your kind remembrance of me through your presents of game—they remind me of my youthful days when I often traversed the moors and fields myself, and in a quick and steady aim might have been not an unworthy competitor, even with you" (30). Branwell was something of a shot and he and Willy Weightman organised pigeon shoots in Haworth, to the disapproval of Emily (plate 19). The famous "Gun Group" painted by Branwell shows him looking highly satisfied, with his gun and a dead bird on the table before him (plate 17). When he was a tutor at Broughton-in-Furness Branwell sent home "A brace of wild ducks, a brace of black grouse, a brace of partridges, ditto of snipe, ditto of curlews, and a large salmon". It may have been such overwhelming gifts that induced Charlotte to write to her friend Ellen "I won't be a cook, I hate cooking".

When the household property was sold up bread tins and bread boards were listed, and also toasting forks (1/9d). The sale also included a bread fleak (2/6d)—this was a rack with short feet which was lowered on to a table and hung with wafer thin pieces of oatcake about 9 inches across and then pulled up to the ceiling and the oatcake left to dry. Oatcake was a food eaten in quantity in the

(29) S.H.B. 591, C.S. 462
(30) B.P.M.

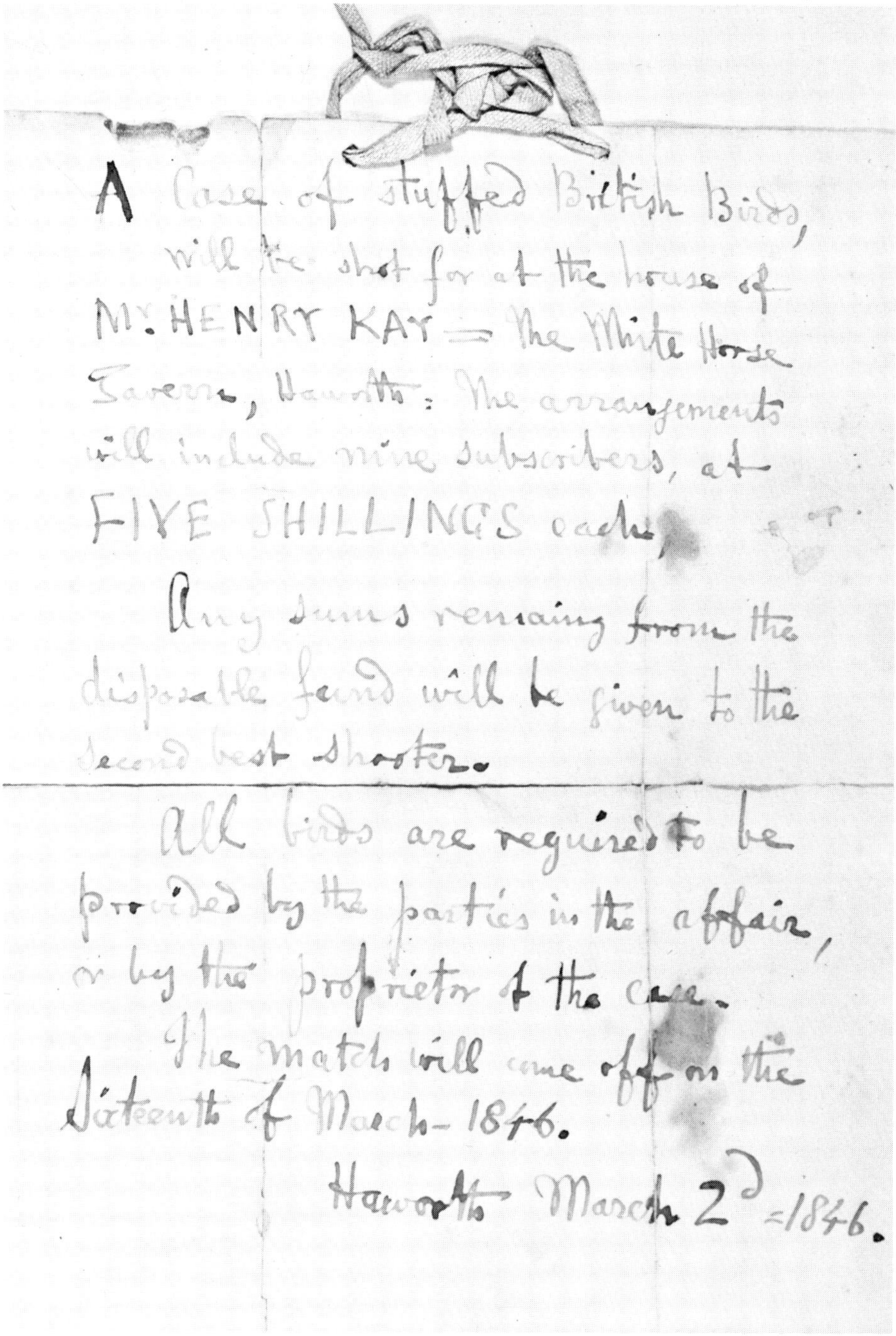

A case of stuffed British Birds,
will be shot for at the house of
Mr. HENRY KAY — the White Horse
Tavern, Haworth: The arrangements
will include nine subscribers, at
FIVE SHILLINGS each,

Any sums remaining from the
disposable fund will be given to the
second best shooter.

All birds are required to be
provided by the parties in the affair,
or by the proprietor of the case.
The match will come off on the
Sixteenth of March — 1846.

Haworth March 2d — 1846.

Plate 19. Branwell Bronte's notice for a Shooting Match.

North of England at a time when wheat for bread was expensive and the native grown oat provided wholesome, cheap nourishment.

Emily helped Sarah Wood with the baking "scribbling on bits of paper in t'kitchen waiting for t'kettle to boil or t'bread to bake". She also studied German during these labours. Professor Hoppin observed the kitchen was "exquisitely neat and the copper pans shone like gold". Monday was baking day and Charlotte must have been helping when she wrote to Ellen that the Keighley curate Mr. Schmidt "had descended on them for tea". Charlotte was not pleased "it was Monday (baking day) and I was hot and tired". The family took breakfast in Mr. Brontë's study at 9.00 a.m. and, as was usual at the time, sometimes visitors were entertained. In September 1851 Mr. Morgan arrived bearing gifts "a lot of tracts" for Charlotte, and stayed for breakfast. (31)

Tea Parties for parishioners and curates were a regular feature of the household routine, and served as useful material for Charlotte's novels. Tea was taken at 6 o'clock and was daintily served in the dining room; dinner was served at 2 o'clock. Charlotte, returning from London in 1853 bringing Ellen Nussey with her, wrote to Martha "the tablecloth had better be put on the dining room *tables*—you will have something prepared that will do for supper——perhaps a nice piece of cold boiled ham would be as well as anything, as it will come in for breakfast in the morning".

Dr. Langley (the Bishop of Ripon who later became Archbishop of Canterbury) came to stay with Charlotte and her father, and there was a great bustle of preparation. In spite of Charlotte's anxiety all went well, Martha waiting at table, and re-inforcements brought in to help in the kitchen; Charlotte writes "All the parsons were invited to tea and stayed to supper!".

Aunt Branwell seems to have skilfully avoided these clerical encounters by taking some of her meals upstairs in her room, though she could tilt an argument at table with the best. She seems to have been a very competent housekeeper and the sisters felt her loss keenly. After her death the running of the house was not to Charlotte's taste, though Mr. Brontë allowed the sisters a free hand in household affairs. There would be much to do in the days when all food was prepared and cooked at home, cakes and bread baked, beer brewed, oat cake made and dried on the rack in the kitchen. Madame Cortazzo points out that Nancy, the servant at the Parsonage, did not find Aunt Branwell as compliant as her ailing sister

(31) The word 'breakfast' was used for any meal early in the day.

Mrs. Brontë had been. Miss Branwell would not allow the servants to fetch their own beer from the cellar as they had done in Mrs. Brontë's time—they must be content with half a pint each, which Miss Branwell insisted on fetching herself. The utensils she used for brewing were sold at the sale in 1861 for 1/-d. As the sale also includes a coffee mill at 1/10d and wine bottles (1doz. at 1/10d) and four decanters for 5/-d it seems beer was not the only beverage consumed. A tea urn, no doubt pressed into use for parish teas, was sold for 17/-d.

Pets and Painting

The Brontës amused themselves with a variety of pastimes when they were not engaged in reading. They were fond of music and gathered round the piano with their friends to sing, possibly accompanied by Branwell on his violin. They owned a card table and played chess,. The girls employed their leisure in making small embroidered articles as gifts for their friends and many examples of their hand work are to be seen at the Museum.

Clearly, one of their favourite occupations was painting, and a Keighley sign-writer, John Bradley, gave them lessons. Branwell was considered to have some talent and was sent to William Robinson, a well-known Leeds artist, for lessons. He left a legacy of oil portraits and sketches which show more of the character of the painter than the sitter. The portraits at the Museum show a certain wild-eyed melancholia, reflecting more of what he felt than what he saw. Painting was fashionable at this period, and the sisters spent many hours copying in minute detail the work of other artists from engravings and books. Charlotte read Ruskin's works and expressed a liking for Modern Painters and the idea of the Seven Lamps (32). She wrote to W. S. Williams, her publisher, congratulating him on the approaching publication of Ruskin's works. (33)

Some of the favourite subjects of the sisters were the family pets of which they had an interesting variety. Mr. Brontë and his daughters were animal lovers of a practical kind as, not only did they write about their pets, but took time and trouble over their well-being, and showed a remarkable talent for rearing wild birds in captivity. Mr. Brontë, brought up in a farming community, had a great affection for all animals, either wild or domestic. Practical considerations also weighed with him, a "house dog" would be a necessity in the rough days in which he lived when each man must protect his own. His house would be safer from the miscreants against whom he kept his pistols loaded overnight; and his daughters could take their long walks across the moors accompanied by a dog the size of Keeper, or with the keen eye of Grasper. According to their portraits, drawn by the sisters, neither dog was of the kind to be

(32) S.H.B. 588, C.S. 461
(33) S.H.B. 438, C.S. 346

crossed. Keeper's collar, on exhibition at the Museum, shows him to have been a dog of powerful build, and Grasper's picture shows him a keen dog well able to live up to his name. The affection of the Brontë family for all birds and animals, whether wild or domestic, is shown in their drawings and writings, many on exhibition at the Museum.

In 1843 Anne was given a Blenheim spaniel, Flossy, by the Robinsons of Thorp Green, and two charming pictures by Charlotte are on view at the Museum (plate 20). Emily also drew a sketch of Flossy lying beside Keeper, who has a cat between his paws. Flossy was devoted to Anne and loved to lie on the settee when Aunt Branwell's eye was not on her. She had a large litter of puppies, one of which was given to Ellen Nussey and, according to Charlotte, "behaved abominably" making her bed in Ellen's best bonnet box.

Grasper was an Irish terrier, the house dog, for which Mr. Brontë paid tax in 1831—he was "the master's dog" and Emily sketched his head in January 1834. His place was taken by Keeper (plate 21) the tawny puppy whom Charlotte described as standing in the kitchen "like a devouring flame". He grew up to be a dog of massive proportions and seems to have had mastiff blood in him, and attached himself to Emily who well knew how to deal with him. It was Keeper who was punished by Emily for lying on her white bed, and he joined the mourners at her funeral; he lived a long life, dying in December 1851. Charlotte wrote to Ellen "Keeper died last Monday morning . . . Flossy is dull and misses him". Flossy died obese, and full of years, in 1854.

In 1855 Mr. Brontë's notebook has an entry "bought Plato from Mr. Summerscales for £3-0-od. Plato is a breed from a Newfoundland bitch and a water spaniel of Mr. Ferrand". Mr. Ferrand was the Bingley friend who was a generous supplier of game for the Brontës' larder. After Mr. Brontë died Mr. Nicholls took Plato with him to Ireland, where he lived to be thirteen years of age.

A succession of household cats is on record, two, Black Tom and Tiger—being mentioned by Charlotte. She wrote "the poor little cat is dead—Emily *is* sorry". This was Black Tom. Emily must have been adept at dealing with animals and birds as she successfully reared Hero, the hawk, who was found on the moors as an injured fledgling. Her painting of Hero in the Bonnell collection may have been a copy of a drawing in Audubon's book of birds of which there

Plate 20. 'Flossy' a watercolour by Charlotte.

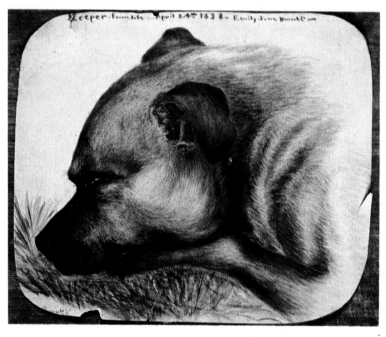

Plate 21. 'Keeper' drawn by Emily.

Plate 22. Three patterns designed by Charlotte.

Plate 23. Pattern of Wallpaper found in Branwell's room.

was a copy at the Parsonage. A canary called Dick lived in a cage in the dining room, and other pets of unknown varieties joined the household at intervals, including Rainbow, Jasper and Diamond. Anne's Diary records "Got a wild goose which has flown away, and three tame ones, one of which was killed".

Apparently Aunt Branwell found this accumulation of pets too much for her, for, in the absence of the sisters, she must have felt compelled to take action. Anne had gone to Thorp Green, Emily and Charlotte to Brussels, but on their return they were grieved to find that the number sadly reduced. Emily's Diary tells "lost the hawk, Hero, which with the geese was given away and is doubtless dead, for when I came home from Brussels I enquired on all hands and could hear nothing of him". Victoria and Adelaide, the geese, were "housed in the peathouse" which stood at the top of the back garden near the wall. There is no indication that there was ever a horse at the Parsonage. Mr. Brontë seemed to have been a great walker.

Emily's first task of the day was to feed the pets and give the dogs a dish of oatmeal. The last task of her life was to go into the back kitchen for bread and meat for her beloved dogs. Returning from Scarborough, where Anne had died, Charlotte wrote "Keeper may visit Emily's little bedroom—as he still does day by day, and Flossy may look wistfully round for Anne. They will never see them again, —nor shall I".

Epilogue

Written records of building work done at the Parsonage are few, and only the small crumbs in letters and note books of the Brontës are available evidence.

As with many old houses, the Parsonage must have seen many changes since it was built in 1778. It is hoped that some day a picture or document will come to light giving an accurate record of the original house.

Most of the descriptions we have are based on information given after 1860 and should be judged with this in mind. The second half of the 19th century enjoyed a prosperity greater than the first which was a time of political upheaval. Charlotte was enchanted by her visits to the Great Exhibition of 1851 held at the Crystal Palace. The new era of industrial achievements astonished and delighted her. The fashion of denigrating the Exhibition as a vulgar display of wealth has no place in Charlotte's account of her visit—she had outgrown envy. "Yesterday I went for the second time to the Crystal Palace. We remained in it about three hours, and I must say I was more struck with it on this occasion than at my first visit. It is a wonderful place, vast, strange, new, and impossible to describe . . . whatever human industry has created, you find there . . . from railway engines . . . to the glass-covered and velvet-spread stands loaded with the most gorgeous work of the goldsmith . . . fair as Eastern genii might have created. It seems as if magic only could have gathered this mass of wealth from all the ends of the earth—as if none but supernatural hands could have arranged it thus, with such a blaze and contrast of colours and marvellous power of effect" (34). The elaborate rooms heavily hung with velvet and lace which formed a background to the homes of the writers of the late nineteenth century were in marked contrast to the simple home of the Brontës.

Mrs. Gaskell, a successful and prosperous writer of fiction, was full of admiration for Charlotte, though not quite so enthusiastic about some other members of the family. She painted a picture in words (some of which she was later to regret) of the Brontës and their

(34) S.H.B. 674. C.S. 514

background, aware that in order to portray the heroine as whiter than white a sombre backcloth would serve her purpose to advantage. A tyrannical father, reprobate brother, oppressive school and grinding poverty are all set in a grim landscape. Ever since Mrs. Gaskell's day many writers on the Brontës have accepted the background she drew as fact, making no allowance for artistic licence, but, as Mr. Brontë observed, the public as a whole prefer melodrama. Visitors to the Parsonage will make their own assessment—what they seek they will find—and surely not judge the living standards of the Brontës by that of our own time. Our own time could be equally harshly judged by those in the future whose standard will again be different from our own.

That the Brontës, particularly Emily, loved their home is clear from their writings. There are many references in Charlotte's letters indicating her longing to be at home when she was away, a natural reaction, but one to Ellen Nussey when Charlotte was going to teach at Roe Head is more telling "Yes, I am going to teach in the very school where I myself was taught—I am sad—very sad at the thought of leaving home". Emily was never happy away from home and cut short her sojourn at Roe Head in order to return to Haworth. Anne's poem "Home", written probably while she was at Thorp Green, sounds a similar note—

> "*Restore to me that little spot,*
> *with grey walls compassed round*
>
> . . .
>
> *Oh give me back my home*"!

Perhaps Charlotte drew the best picture herself of her life at home in her letter to Emily written from Brussels in 1843. "This is Sunday morning—they are at their idolatrous 'Messe' and I am here in the refectoire—I should like uncommonly to be in the dining room at home, or in the kitchen, or in the back kitchen—I should like to be cutting up the hash, with the Clerk and some registry people at the other table, and you standing by watching that I put enough flour and not too much pepper and that above all I save the best pieces of the leg of mutton for Tiger and Keeper, the first of which personages would be jumping about the dish and carving knife, and the latter standing like a devouring flame on the kitchen floor . . . I pray with all my heart and soul that all may continue well at

Haworth; above all in our grey half inhabited house . . . GOD
BLESS THE WALLS THEREOF".

> The house is old, the trees are bare
> And moonless bends the misty dome
> But what on earth is half so dear,
> So longed for as the hearth of home?

Emily Brontë.

William Wood's Accounts

The following are extracts from the account book of William Wood, Joiner, of Haworth. They include the charge for the coffins etc. of Miss Branwell, Branwell, and Emily. Note the charge of 5/-d for papering and sizing a room in 1843. William Wood was the joiner to whom Charlotte gave the order to make new furniture when she refurbished the Parsonage.

1832	P. BRONTY			
June 15	To 2 frames		7/-.	
Aug. 23	by cash	10/-.		
Sept. 3	To frame & glass		2/-.	
Nov. 29	To 1 frame & glass		4/-.	
Dec. 13	by cash	10/6.		
Dec. 17	To 2 strichers		2/8d.	*Stretchers for chairs.*
1837	P. BRONTY			
	To 1 cord		1/-.	
	To 1 stricher		8.	
	To 1 door		2/4.	
Oct. 22	To 1 picter frame		4/3d.	
	Settled W.W. 1837			
Jan. 4th	3 stretcher		4/-.	
	To 1 chair repearing		2/-.	
Aug. 12	To pinna forte repay		2/2.	*Pianoforte repairing.*
	To 2 gun rods		9/2.	
Dec. 1	1 Cuberd lock		1/-d.	*Cupboard*
1839	Rev. P. B. Bronty			
Dec. 23	To 6 chaires with air botoms		£3/18/-.	*Hair seats.*
1842	Rev. P. Bronty M.A.			
	To window blinds repearing		1/6.	
Apr. 20	Rowlers repear		3d.	*Rollers for the clothes mangle (sold for £1/9/-d)*
	Pistol stock		£1/1/-.	
1843	P. Bronty—MINISTER			
Mar. 7	To 1 aster frame repay		9d.	*Haster—a screen to reflect heat when spit-roasting. (Sold for 2/-d at the sale in 1861).*

Mar. 16	To 1 winter edg. do	3/–.	*Winter Hedge—clothes horse. (Sold as above for 10d.).*
	To 1 box repearing	5d.	
May	To 1 rom papring and sise	5/–.	*Room papering and sizing. Cupboard hinges.*
Jul. 18	To cubert enges & sashes		
Aug. 29	To 1 picte frame	7d.	*Picture frame.*
		3/–.	
1844			
Jan. 7	To 1 lock & winter edg repearing	8d.	
	To 1 box	5/–.	
	Settled Wm. Wood		
	P. Bronty		
June 8	To 1 doore repearing	2/9d.	
	To 1 threshold	1/–.	*Threshold.*
	To 3 chairs do	1/2.	
1845	**P. Bronty—Minester**		
Mar. 12	To well cover	8d.	
May 29	To 1 chaire repearing	2d.	
	To 1 chair repearing	6d.	
June 3	To 2 beadsteads repearing	8d.	
June 19	To 1 chair & harme covering	5/–.	*Arm chair.*
July 15	To sash repearing	4d.	
Sept. 21	To 2 sasher hangers	1/8.	
Oct. 14	To 2 of do repearing	1/6d.	
Nov. 24	To 1 chaire repearing	6d.	
1847	**P. Bronty**		
June 10	To 2 doors repearing & other jobs	1/6d.	
	To clock case do	1/–d.	
	To 1 cover for the sugh	1/–d.	*Cover for the soakaway.*
June 30	To 1 box repearing	8d.	
Sept. 18	To temes repearing	3d.	*An old name for a sieve.*
1848	**P. Bronty—MINISTER**		
March	To 1 stir frame repearing		*Stair frame.*
	To 1 winter edg do	9d.	
	To 1 box repearing	5d.	
April 6	To 1 close pole	2/2d.	*Clothes pole.*
July 18	To 1 cubert eng setting on	7d.	*Cupboard hinge fixing.*
Aug. 23	To 1 picter frame	3/–d.	
Aug. 28	To cubert repearing		
	To 2 knobs to. 1 esp	1/–d.	
Sept. 24	To 13 yards of sash cord	1/1d.	

1848			
Jan. 7	To 1 chair repearing	1/6d.	
April 6	To 1 close pole	2/2d.	
Aug. 28	To cubert repearing		
	To 2 knobs to esp	1/–d	
Sept. 21	To 2 sasher hanger	1/8d	*Window sashes.*
1849	RVE. P. Bronty		
Jan. 14	Bead repearing	8d.	
Jan. 20	Locks repearing	9d.	
	To 1 door boult ole fitting in door plats	1/6d	*Bolt hole.*
	To 1 handle repearing	1/–d.	
May 31	To repearing & doore plate	6d.	
Jul. 7	To 1 hub & ey fitting on	3d.	*Door staple & eye.*
Aug. 4	To 1 peggy repearing	6d.	*Peggy stick for washing clothes in a tub.*
Oct. 12	To bead lathes	2d.	*Bed laths.*
Oct. 19	To bead head boord	1/–.	*Bed head board.*
Oct. 20	To showr-bath 2 knobs	2/6d	
	Rev. Nickles		
Nov. 16	Rosewood frames	4/–.	
1850	The Trusteys of the Church		
	Window shutren		*Shutters.*
	Wood for citchen		*Kitchen.*
	REV. P. Bronty		
June 15	To furneter removing ½ day	1/9d.	
	Window rouler & rack	1/–.	
	1 set of stand steps	5/9.	
Jan. 16	1 Brush Shaft	4½d.	
Mar. 6	To 1 doore repearing	8d.	
	To 1 sash hanger with cord	8d.	
	To peer glass & tray repearing	2d.	*Pier glass (mirror).*
Mar. 11	To 1 lock fitting on	9d.	
1851	P. Bronty		
June	1 towell stand	1/–.	
	To 8 chair bottoms covering with hair stuffing	18/–.	
	Bookcase	8/–.	
	1 wash and stand	£3/8/–.	
1852			
July	To 1 doore repearing etc.	2/–.	
	Chist of Maghney Droyers		*Chest of mahogany drawers.*

1853

| | Buffhet | | *Stool.* |
| | To 5 cid scins | £1/8/9. | *Kid skins.* |

1855 Feb. 5	Rev. P. Brontey		
	Clothes pole		
	Prive seat		*Privy seat.*
Mar. 29	To 1 sash 18ft. to fitting up	10/6.	

| 1858 | REV. P. Bronty | | |
| | Heve spout | | *Eave spout.* |

| 1860 | REV. P. Bronty | | |
| | To 4 chaires repearing tabel etc | 2/8. | |

| 1861 Jan. | REV. P. Bronty | | |
| | To 1 chair & tabel repearing | 2/2. | |

| 1863 Jan. 14 | REV. J. WADE | | |
| | Many repairs | | |

APPENDIX 2

Extracts from the catalogue of the sale which took place October 1st and 2nd 1861 after Mr. Brontë's death.   (B.S.T. Vol. 14, Part 75 (1965)

Brewing utensils	2/–d
Bed hangings	12/–d
Card Table	12/6d
Piano forte	£ 5/ 5/–d
Bell pulls and pistol	9/–d
Carpets	£ 1/–/–d
Carpets	£ 1/16/–d
Hearth rug	7/6d
Carpet	15/6d
Mah. drawers	£ 2/ 7/–d
6 lots rugs and carpets	£25/ 3/–d
Stair carpet	6/3d
Clock in oak case	£ 1/ 1/–d
Chimney glass (overmantel mirror)	£ 3/ –/–d
Sofa	£ 3/12/–d
6 Mah. chairs	£ 5/ 2/–d
,, dining table	£ 5/ –/–d
Carpet & stool	
Cornice & curtain	